Kinds of Giving: from the Holy Scriptures

Chris A. Legebow

ISBN-978-1-988914-05-3

DEDICATION

I dedicate this book to those who would desire to do something for God so that He might be magnified in your life. May God use you to give as He prospers you, so may you bless others.

Chris Legebow

CONTENTS

Acknowledgments i

1 Introduction to Giving 1

2 Tithing 14

3 Alms 25

4 Sowing a Seed 32

5 Thanksgiving Offering 43

6 Free will Offering 49

7 Vow 55

8 First fruit Offering 66

9 Conclusion 72

Prayers 76

ACKNOWLEDGMENTS

All Scripture taken from Bible Gateway.com
Modern English version (MEV)

1 INTRODUCTION

Chapter 1
Introduction – Giving

Giving is a normal part of a Christian life. We give because God is a giver. God's desire is to prosper His people. SHALOM means complete wholeness – nothing missing. God's people spoke this word to each other regularly. God's servants always had more than enough. They had more than enough so they could give and give generously. God's desire for us is that we would have more than enough of all things so that we could give generously to the preaching of Christ. God's wants us also to give to others. There are different types of giving mentioned in the scriptures. First, we will establish that truly it is God's will for you to live prosperously in body, soul and spirit. It is God's desire to bless his people in every area of their lives. He expresses it throughout His covenants but especially with Abraham and Moses, finally, also through the New Testament of Jesus blood shed for us.

Abraham

God promised Abraham that he would have an inheritance of children who would be so many it would be as stars in the star in number. God promised to bless those who would bless him and fight against those who would fight against him. God made a covenant with Abraham, a promise that God would be with him and prosper him, physically, financially, spiritually.

With God's Word, Abraham left all that he knew from UR of the Chaldees to go to the place God promised to bring him. There is no mention that God appeared to God only that he spoke to him. Abraham was willing to obey God. It took faith to believe that God would direct his paths.

Genesis 12: 2 I will make of you a great nation;
   I will bless you
and make your name great,
   so that you will be a blessing.

3 I will bless them who bless you
   and curse him who curses you,[a]
and in you all families of the earth
   will be blessed."

Abraham and his wife were in their 70's but they obeyed God. Lot his nephew desired to go with them. Abraham let him come. Abraham brought his sheep and goats. God multiplied them in number. Lot prospered because of Abraham. At one point the herds were so many that Lot's servants started fighting over the flocks – both of them claiming some of the herd. Lot, desiring money more than family peace, speaks with Abraham that they must separate because of the issue about keeping track of the herds.

Abraham who was a man of peace cared more about preserving family piece than about the numbers of the herds. Abraham had God's Word that God would prosper him. He was not covetousness even though he was very prosperous. He let Lot choose the direction he wanted to go. Lot saw the abundant water and rich valley and chose it, not caring about what would happen to his uncle or his flocks. Right after Lot's departure, God speaks with Abraham once more to confirm his covenant. God tells Abraham to lift up his eyes to see the land and that every place he sees, God will give it unto him. God promises him more than simply one spot but a 360 degree of ownership. He promises that his seed will be as numerous as dust in the earth.

Genesis 13: 14 After Lot had departed from him, the Lord said to Abram, "Lift up now your eyes, and look from the place where you are, northward and southward and eastward and westward. 15 All the land that you see I will give to you and to your descendants forever. 16 I will make your descendants like the dust of the earth, so that if a man could number the dust of the earth, then your descendants could also be numbered. 17 Arise, and walk throughout the land across its length and its width, for I will give it to you."

It took about 30 years for the fulfillment of God's promise to Abraham of having an heir. God prospered him abundantly throughout. He even had a child of his wife's servant Hagar. God promised that he and Sarah would have a child that would be the child of promise. God's promise to Abraham is the Abrahamic covenant. There are two parts to a covenant. The first part is what God promised; the other part is what Abraham must do to inherit the promises and receive God's blessing. It was a most serious thing; God Told him that as a sign of his agreement with the covenant that he was to be circumcised and that all the males in his blood line were to be circumcised. It required total obedience. Abraham obeyed.

Genesis 17: 9 Then God said to Abraham, "As for you, you shall keep My covenant, you and your descendants after you throughout their generations. 10 This is My covenant, which you shall keep, between Me and you and your descendants after you; every male among you shall be circumcised. 11 You shall circumcise the flesh of your foreskins, and it shall be a sign of the covenant between Me and you. 12 Every male throughout every generation that is eight days old shall be circumcised, whether born in your household or bought with money from a foreigner who is not your descendant. 13 He who is born in your house and he who is bought with your money must be circumcised. My covenant shall be in your flesh as an everlasting covenant. 14 Any uncircumcised male whose flesh of his foreskin is not circumcised shall be cut off from his people. He has broken My covenant."

God also promised that his wife Sarah would have the child even though they were both nearly 100 years old. It seemed impossible but God made it very clear that Sarah's name was to be Sarah not Sarai and that she would bear the child. You must realize that God's promise was a miracle. Sarah had never been able to have children even while she was of age to have them; believing that God could give them children while they were centenarians was supernatural faith.

Genesis 17: 15 Then God said to Abraham, "As for Sarai your wife, you will not call her name Sarai, but her name will be Sarah. 16 I will bless her and also give you a son by her. I will bless her, and she will be the mother of nations. Kings of peoples will come from her."

17 Then Abraham fell on his face and laughed and said in his heart, "Shall a child be born to a man that is a hundred years old? Shall Sarah, who is ninety years old, bear a child?" 18 Abraham said to God, "Oh, that Ishmael might live before You!"

Genesis 17: 19 Then God said, "No, but your wife Sarah will bear you a son, and you will call his name Isaac. I will establish My covenant with him as an everlasting covenant and with his descendants after him. 20 And as for Ishmael, I have heard you. I have blessed him, and will make him fruitful and will multiply him exceedingly. He will be the father of twelve princes, and I will make him a great nation. 21 But I will establish My covenant with Isaac, whom Sarah will bear to you at this set time next year." 22 Then He stopped talking with Abraham, and God went up from him.

Soon after, God sent angels in human disguise to speak to Abraham. They promised that within a year, Abraham's son would be born. Sarah overheard and laughed. Truly it seems to be miraculous. Within the next year she did have the child Isaac. Through him came a lineage of believers who honoured God. Through Isaac came Jacob renamed Israel who had 12 sons who because the foundations of the nation Israel in 12 tribes. God kept his covenant.

Genesis 18: 13 Then the Lord said to Abraham, "Why did Sarah laugh and say, 'Shall I surely bear a child when I am old?' 14 Is anything too difficult for the Lord? At the appointed time I will return to you, at this time next year, and Sarah will have a son."

Moses

God's promise to Moses was that God would use Moses to lead Israel out of Egyptian bondage. Israel had become slaves of the Egyptians for 400 years. Moses did not believe he could do it alone, so God allowed his brother Aaron to assist him. This is not a teaching on the events of Moses only a mention of the covenant God made with Moses and through him with Israel.

Moses and Aaron went to Egypt to demand the people of Israel free because it was God's Command. The Pharaoh's heart was hard and did not believe in God. Through a series of judgements on Egypt – horrible plagues – finally culminating the death of Pharaoh's son, Pharaoh let them go free. Moses led about 2 million Israelites out of Egypt. God brought them to the Red Sea. Pharaoh, sent his army after them to kill them all. As the Egyptians had Israel against the Red Sea, God miraculously manifested in their midst. He appeared to defend Israel.

Exodus 14: 19 Then the angel of God, which went before the camp of Israel, moved and went behind them, and the pillar of the cloud moved before them and stood behind them. 20 So it came between the camp of the Egyptians and the camp of Israel, and there was a cloud and darkness to them, but it gave light by night.

God commanded Moses to stretch out his rod over the Red Sea and it would part. He did. It parted. Moses led Israel through the midst of the Red Sea. After the last Israelite was safe, God released the waters and the Egyptians chasing them to drown. Moses through the people to Mount Sinai as God had instructed him to do. It was there God gathered them so they could receive the commandments of God. God instructed Moses to come up the mountain. There was thunder and lightning upon the mountain top. The people were not to approach the mountain but to wait for Moses to return.

Exodus 19: 7 So Moses came and called for the elders of the people and laid before them all these words which the Lord commanded him. 8 Then all the people answered together and said, "All that the Lord has spoken we will do." And Moses brought back the words of the people to the Lord.

9 The Lord said to Moses, "Indeed, I am going to come to you in a thick cloud, so that the people may

God spoke with Moses as a friend speaks to a friend. Truly God had kept the first part of His covenant. He delivered Israel out of Egypt after 400 years. It is miraculous. God gave Moses commandments. These commandments were given so that Israel would know right from wrong. Israel had not been free in 400 years. God's commandments were given to guide people in living a pleasing life unto God. God wrote the commandments on the side of the mountain with his finger. He carved two huge stone tablets with the commandments on them. He was to give these commandments to Israel and instruct them to keep and treasure these words because it was God's covenant with them. If they would honour God and keep the commandments, God would bless them and multiply them and give them the land that was promised to Abraham. It was a keeping of God's covenant with Abraham as well as a promise to them. This book is not a detailed teaching on the commandments of God but I list them for clarity.

God's Commandments

Exodus 20: 1 Now God spoke all these words, saying:

2 I am the Lord your God, who brought you out of the land of Egypt, out of the house of bondage.

3 You shall have no other gods before Me.

4 You shall not make for yourself any graven idol, or any likeness of anything that is in heaven above, or that is in the earth beneath, or that is in the water below the earth. 5 You shall not bow down to them or serve them; for I, the Lord your God, am a jealous God, visiting the iniquity of the fathers on the children to the third and fourth generation of them who

hate Me, 6 and showing lovingkindness to thousands of them who love Me and keep My commandments.

7 You shall not take the name of the Lord your God in vain, for the Lord will not hold guiltless anyone who takes His name in vain.

8 Remember the Sabbath day and keep it holy. 9 Six days you shall labor and do all your work, 10 but the seventh day is a Sabbath to the Lord your God. On it you shall not do any work, you, or your son, or your daughter, or your male servant, or your female servant, or your livestock, or your sojourner who is within your gates. 11 For in six days the Lord made heaven and earth, the sea, and all that is in them, and rested on the seventh day. Therefore the Lord blessed the Sabbath day and made it holy.

12 Honor your father and your mother, that your days may be long in the land which the Lord your God is giving you.

13 You shall not murder.

14 You shall not commit adultery.

15 You shall not steal.

16 You shall not bear false witness against your neighbor.

17 You shall not covet your neighbor's house; you shall not covet your neighbor's wife, or his manservant, or his maidservant, or his ox, or his donkey, or anything that is your neighbor's.

Truly these were God's own words. Keeping these words would mean peace with God and living in the blessings of God. Not keeping these words would mean sinning against God. Later God revealed other Levitical laws to Moses a total of 613. Aaron's descendants became teaching priests and servants of God by heritage.

Israel

Israel did not hearken to God's commandments. They doubted God, complained, conspired to kill Moses and Aaron more than once. Israel was not living by the commandments. It must have been tough for Moses to lead Israel but he did and he keep interceding for Israel and praying for them when they sinned. His prayers and Aron's and the other priests' prayers stopped plagues and deaths because God judged Israel for being hard hearted and plotting to kill God's anointed prophet. Israel's disobedience and sin, caused them to wander in the wilderness for 40 years until the last of the corrupt people had died. Even though God judged Israel, He still provided food in the form of manna, a bread like substance. God provided in the desert by it spurting from a rock. God allowed their clothing and their shoes to be preserved so they had no lack.

In one instance, Moses sinned. Even though God had done all these things for Israel, they desired water. Rather than request for God to provide they grumbled against Moses. They were completely unbelieving and complained that Moses was to blame. God had instructed Moses to speak to the rock, to sing to the rock. God gave different instructions on different occasions. God told him to speak to the rock that water might spring up. Whenever God had instructed God in the past, Moses obeyed and God provided. Moses was angry at Israel and their unbelief. Anyone can sympathize with them after reading of his leadership experience with them. On this one occasion, Moses disobeyed. Rather than speak to the rock, he hit the rock and used harsh words reproving Israel for their unbelief (Exodus 20). Because of it Moses was judged and not allowed to go into the promised land although he was permitted to view it.

Finally, after 40 years of wandering in the wilderness, Israel approached the sights of the promised land. It was here that God gave special instructions to Moses. He spoke strong words to give to Israel so that they may live long lives and be prosperous. They were to study, memorize and teach to their children the commandments and keep them. If they would keep them, God would truly keep His covenant with them to multiply them, their families, their herds, all within their spheres of influence. Clearly it is God's desire to bless Israel. I would recommend reading all the book of Deuteronomy for study purposes but I list only a slice of the promises of blessings here.

Covenant promises

Deuteronomy 28: 8 The Lord will send a blessing on your barns and on everything you put your hand to. The Lord your God will bless you in the land he is giving you.

9 The Lord will establish you as his holy people, as he promised you on oath, if you keep the commands of the Lord your God and walk in obedience to him. 10 Then all the peoples on earth will see that you are called by the name of the Lord, and they will fear you. 11 The Lord will grant you abundant prosperity—in the fruit of your womb, the young of

your livestock and the crops of your ground—in the land he swore to your ancestors to give you.

12 The Lord will open the heavens, the storehouse of his bounty, to send rain on your land in season and to bless all the work of your hands. You will lend to many nations but will borrow from none. 13 The Lord will make you the head, not the tail. If you pay attention to the commands of the Lord your God that I give you this day and carefully follow them, you will always be at the top, never at the bottom. 14 Do not turn aside from any of the commands I give you today, to the right or to the left, following other gods and serving them.

You may believe those promises are only for Israel. It would be true if Jesus Christ did not come to fulfill all the Messianic prophecies and all the laws of God. Jesus lived a Holy life. Jesus died for our sins so that if we would believe in Him – that he died for our sins – we would have eternal life with God. The hope of living in with God always is special on its own but that is not the extent of the blessing. Because Jesus never sinned, all the promises of Abraham and all the promises of Moses are ours by faith in Jesus Christ. By faith we receive the blessings of all the covenants of God.

As Abraham believed God, so we also can by faith believe in the Lord Jesus Christ and receive the blessings of the covenant. It requires faith. It also requires living in covenant with God.

Romans 4: 3 What does the Scripture say? "Abraham believed God, and it was credited to him as righteousness."[a]

Romans 4: 18 Against all hope, he believed in hope, that he might become the father of many nations according to what was spoken, "So shall your descendants be."[d] 19 And not being weak in faith, he did not consider his own body to be dead (when he was about a hundred years old), nor yet the deadness of Sarah's womb. 20 He did not waver at the promise of God through unbelief, but was strong in faith, giving glory to God, 21 and being fully persuaded that what God had promised, He was able to perform. 22 Therefore "it was credited to him as righteousness."[e] 23 Now the words, "it was credited to him," were not written for his sake only, 24 but also for us, to whom it shall be credited if we believe in Him who raised Jesus our Lord from the dead, 25 who was delivered for our transgressions, and was raised for our justification.

Believing in Jesus requires that we live for God. We honour Him by praise and worship. We honour Him by studying the scriptures. We keep

God's Word as a priority and Keep God first in our lives. Believing in Jesus, gives us access to God as the Holy Spirit lives on the inside of us. God's Spirit leads us and guides us. The Holy Spirit teaches us and corrects us.

John 14: 16 I will pray the Father, and He will give you another Counselor, that He may be with you forever: 17 the Spirit of truth, whom the world cannot receive, for it does not see Him, neither does it know Him. But you know Him, for He lives with you, and will be in you.

John 14: 25 "I have spoken these things to you while I am still with you. 26 But the Counselor, the Holy Spirit, whom the Father will send in My name, will teach you everything and remind you of all that I told you.

If we confess our sins, Jesus will forgive us. It will be just as if we never sinned (1 John 1:9). Jesus shed blood cleanses us from all sin and iniquity. It doesn't mean we should sin because we can always get forgiveness. It means we should be desiring to know God more. His Holy presence is within us, strengthens, encourages and transforms us from glory to glory. True Christians are not trying to find ways to sin; true Christians are trying to live their lives wholly unto God.

1 Corinthians 3: 18 But we all, seeing the glory of the Lord with unveiled faces, as in a mirror, are being transformed into the same image from glory to glory by the Spirit of the Lord.

God's Spirit on the inside of us, changes us so that we resemble God. His character is in us. It is a true Christian who is living in covenant relationship with God that is my audience. There are different types of giving in a Christian's life. I will explain various types of giving in my book. A brief summary of the types follows.

Giving

The first thing God teaches us is to that God desires to bless us so that we can give to others. He wants to give us so much that we want to sow into others' lives. It is stewardship. Once you realize that God delights in giving you your heart's desires, your view of God is transformed. You desire to live wholly unto God knowing that He gives you the best. It is not normal for carnal man to give; there is something about the fleshly person that covets and does not consider anyone else. Learning that God is a giver and prospers us so that we can be givers is a starting point for us spiritually. Many people do not consider financial giving to be spiritual but it is an expression of worship to God and it keeps the commandments of loving

God with all your heart, and loving your neighbour as yourself.

Acts 20: 35 I have shewed you all things, how that so labouring ye ought to support the weak, and to remember the words of the Lord Jesus, how he said, It is more blessed to give than to receive.

Tithes

In most full gospel churches, there is some kind of teaching for people new to the church outside of the Sunday services. It may be called a membership class, or a faith class etc. It usually covers the foundations of the Christian faith as well as information about the church itself and becoming a member. Tithing will be taught as part of a normal part of being a Christian. Tithing means literally giving 10% of your increase or your income to God. Many people resist this teaching at first. The reason they resist it is covetousness or ignorance. Studying the benefits of tithing and God's commandment to do it are covered in that chapter.

Mal 3: 10 Bring ye all the tithes into the storehouse, that there may be meat in mine house, and prove me now herewith, saith the LORD of hosts, if I will not open you the windows of heaven, and pour you out a blessing, that there shall not be room enough to receive it.

Alms

Alms or giving to the poor is important. God commanded it. Those who have more than enough should care for those who have nothing. It's right because God commanded it so we should do it, but there are also special blessings upon people who do give to the poor. The Israelites were commanded to care for the poor by leaving some parts of their crops for those who had nothing. Family members were commanded to care for other family members. In the new testament, The Church cared for widows and orphans.

Matt 26: 11 For ye have the poor always with you; but me ye have not always.

Matt 25: 40 And the King shall answer and say unto them, Verily I say unto you, Inasmuch as ye have done it unto one of the least of these my brethren, ye have done it unto me.

There are special opportunities that come in a person's life. It may be because God prompts you in a special way. Those with the gift of giving often have God speak to them directing them to give to certain people. Sometimes, God gives a specific amount and the person obeys. What results is often answers to prayer to the receiver.

Sowing a seed

There are specific occasions when a person requires an answer to prayer. The person prays, usually for something that is impossible in the natural. The person will give a gift of finances to God through a specific ministry or church and wrap his or her faith around it. What occurs is that God honours the person's giving in faith for the miracle and special favour is released on the person's faith. There is a resistance to many people to the teaching on sowing a seed. Just as there is a release of enlightenment to cause a person to know that God wants to financially bless you, just as there is more understanding once a person begins to know the benefits of tithing, there is a dimension of seed giving that releases special blessings towards a person's life. It is a different type of giving as are the rewards.

– Ecclesiastes 11:
1Cast thy bread upon the waters: for thou shalt find it after many days.
2Give a portion to seven, and also to eight; for thou knowest not what evil shall be upon the earth.
3If the clouds be full of rain, they empty themselves upon the earth: and if the tree fall toward the south, or toward the north, in the place where the tree falleth, there it shall be.
4He that observeth the wind shall not sow; and he that regardeth the clouds shall not reap.
5As thou knowest not what is the way of the spirit, nor how the bones do grow in the womb of her that is with child: even so thou knowest not the works of God who maketh all.
6In the morning sow thy seed, and in the evening withhold not thine hand: for thou knowest not whether shall prosper, either this or that, or whether they both shall be alike good.
Matt 13: 8But other fell into good ground, and brought forth fruit, some an hundredfold, some sixtyfold, some thirtyfold.

Thanksgiving offerings

As you live with God, you will realize how merciful, giving and excellent that He is in all His ways. As you grow in relationship with God, you are going to start realizing that He gives you not only enough, but more than enough. You're going to start knowing that God gives you your heart's desires. The innermost desires of your heart, God takes pleasure in giving to you. What occurs in your spirit is that you develop an attitude of gratitude. It becomes overwhelming. You will want to show an expression of gratitude to God by special giving. It is your special giving to God because of the way He has blessed you. You desire to give. Sometimes it is much that you give. Sometimes it is celebrated with others.

Leviticus 7: 11And this is the law of the sacrifice of peace offerings, which he shall offer unto the LORD.

12If he offer it for a thanksgiving, then he shall offer with the sacrifice of thanksgiving unleavened cakes mingled with oil, and unleavened wafers anointed with oil, and cakes mingled with oil, of fine flour, fried.

13Besides the cakes, he shall offer for his offering leavened bread with the sacrifice of thanksgiving of his peace offerings.

14And of it he shall offer one out of the whole oblation for an heave offering unto the LORD, and it shall be the priest's that sprinkleth the blood of the peace offerings.

15And the flesh of the sacrifice of his peace offerings for thanksgiving shall be eaten the same day that it is offered; he shall not leave any of it until the morning.

Psalm 100

1Make a joyful noise unto the LORD, all ye lands.

2Serve the LORD with gladness: come before his presence with singing.

3Know ye that the LORD he is God: it is he that hath made us, and not we ourselves; we are his people, and the sheep of his pasture.

4Enter into his gates with thanksgiving, and into his courts with praise: be thankful unto him, and bless his name.

5For the LORD is good; his mercy is everlasting; and his truth endureth to all generations.

Freewill offering

A free will offering is exactly what it says it is. It is giving to God because you will to do it. Often, it means a denomination of money in your wallet. You already gave all your other types of giving, but this gift is extra. It is like giving extra something to your child or your spouse. You don't have to do it. It isn't expected, but you do it.

– Psalm 54: 6I will freely sacrifice unto thee: I will praise thy name, O LORD; for it is good.

First fruits offerings Exodus 35: 29 The children of Israel brought a willing offering unto the LORD, every man and woman, whose heart made them willing to bring for all manner of work, which the LORD had commanded to be made by the hand of Moses.

Making a vow offering

The making of a vow is something very serious and should never be entered into lightly. It is something that could be a serious pledge as serious as your life. If you make a vow to God, you must keep it. God will hold you to your vow. Breaking a vow is a sin. The most common type of vow most people know of is a marriage vow. Those who are Christians that make the vow are pledging their lives to each other and to God. It is a life long vow.

– Leviticus 7: 16But if the sacrifice of his offering be a vow, or a voluntary offering, it shall be eaten the same day that he offereth his sacrifice: and on the morrow also the remainder of it shall be eaten:

First fruits offering

The First fruits offering is a gift of finances to God through certain ministries or churches, where you willingly give a portion of your increase because God has promoted you or you have received new levels of income or prosperity. The first has a special significance to God. You give the amount of the increase. You do it because God is merciful and generous and you desire to give. It is your pleasure to give because you realize all that you are, all that you have, has come to you by the mercy of God.

– Exodus 13:
1And the LORD spake unto Moses, saying,
2Sanctify unto me all the firstborn, whatsoever openeth the womb among the children of Israel, both of man and of beast: it is mine.
First fruits continued – Exodus 22: 29Thou shalt not delay to offer the first of thy ripe fruits, and of thy liquors: the firstborn of thy sons shalt thou give unto me. 30Likewise shalt thou do with thine oxen, and with thy sheep: seven days it shall be with his dam; on the eighth day thou shalt give it me.

Romans 11: 16For if the first fruit be holy, the lump is also holy: and if the root be holy, so are the branches.

2 TITHING

Chapter 2

After I became a Christian, I was in a Church service within a week and the offering was being taken. I didn't have much money. I didn't know about giving to God. I asked my friend if we had to give something. She gave me a proper response. She said I only should give if I want to. I relaxed. I thought to myself, "I don't want to." I wasn't raised in a Christian home. No one had taught me about giving except my mom who taught me giving and giving and giving. She always gave more than what I needed. She would always do more than expected. She was kind, caring not just to us but to all people. She was the standard on giving that I knew. I was no where near her standard. I worked hard for my money and I needed every penny. I would sometimes buy special things for my mother or brother. Mostly I bought only for me. I had the assumption since I had earned my money, it was mine. I believed that it was my efforts alone that would help me through life.

It was several months later, in that same Church, I began giving in spurts. I had not been taught about tithing yet. What happened was the Holy Spirit would prompt me to give. I didn't have much money but I would sometimes give my only 5 dollar bill. I realized that at Church, I was worshipping God with other people who knew God and loved Him. I realized that God was changing me and giving me insight. I realized the teaching was speaking directly into my life and I could learn and use what I was taught. Anyone who preached seemed to be especially speaking to me. I could not simply only take without giving something. No one told me I had to, I had not even been taught about finances but something in my spirit knew that I should give.

Later, as I was studying an in-depth Bible class that lasted 9 months, I was part of a group of about 100 students of all different ethnicities and ages learning about the foundations of the faith. We learned the truth about tithing by studying the scriptures and seeing God's Word. We learned that God was the source of all; God gave us the abilities to use our talents and gifts to earn finances. God was the source. It made sense. I knew I always seemed to get pretty good jobs. Once I knew that God was the source, I realized, I could ask Him for excellent jobs. I knew Him to be kind and merciful and generous.

Tithing

The tithe is 10% of your income. It is the first part of your income that we give to God. We give it to God because it is commanded. God gave the commandments to Moses that Israel should live by. God requires the tithe.

Leviticus 27: 30 Any tithe of the land, whether seed of the land or fruit of the trees, belongs to the Lord. It is holy to the Lord. 31 If a man plans on redeeming some of his tithe, he shall add one-fifth to it. 32 Any tithe of herd or flock, all that passes under the counting staff, the tenth one shall be holy to the Lord. 33 A person shall not differentiate between good or bad, nor shall he make a substitute for it, but if he does, then both it and its substitute shall be holy. It shall not be redeemed.

The Israelites would give 1/10 of their flocks, their increase of their produce, their fruit trees etc. They measured and gave the offering to the Levitical priests. The Levites were a tribe of priests the lineage of Aaron, Moses brother. They were not to work other jobs. God appointed them as special caregivers for the Tabernacle of God's presence and in service to God. They lived from part of the offerings given to them. They had lands appointed by God. They were to collect the tithes and it was explained to Moses in detail what they were to do. They themselves were to give a tithe of their income to God as well. It was God's was of consecrating the Levites and also providing for them so that they had more than enough. They could not own property. They were to live Holy unto God and had many special rules that ordinary people didn't have. My book is not a study on the life of a Levite but it is an interesting study.

Later in Israel God speaks through the prophet Malachi a tough judgement because the people of Israel were not following God or tithing or dealing rightly with God. It is in this passage of scripture that we learn that tithing releases blessings to the giver. God commands the tithes be brought to the place you are being spiritually nourished. Should you bring the tithes, as God requires, God will "open the windows of heaven and pour out a blessing that there is not enough room to receive." What it means is God will guard over you and prosper you. The windows of Heaven are like huge paths to receive from. There will be no obstacle to your prayers. You will be living in the realms of God's protection and covering and part of that covering is financial prosperity.

Malachi 3: 8 Will a man rob God? Yet you have robbed Me.

But you say, "How have we robbed You?"

In tithes and offerings. 9 You are cursed with a curse, your whole nation, for you are robbing Me. 10 Bring all the tithes into the storehouse, that there may be food in My house, and test Me now in this, says the Lord of Hosts, if I will not open for you the windows of heaven and pour out for you a blessing, that there will not be room enough to receive it. 11 I will rebuke the devourer for your sakes, so that it will not destroy the fruit of your ground, and the vines in your field will not fail to bear fruit, says the Lord of Hosts. 12 Then all the nations will call you blessed, for you will be a delightful land, says the Lord of Hosts.

God also promises to "rebuke the devourer". Literally, it means God will fight against your enemies. It is as God spoke to Abraham that He would bless those who bless him and fight against them who fought against him. The devil is the enemy of people because God created us for His glory. He especially hates anyone that serves God at all. All people have the same enemy, but not all people believe it or know it. The devil is the real enemy who will try to destroy human lives by strife, divorce, hatred, violence, addictions etc.

John 10: 10 The thief does not come, except to steal and kill and destroy. I came that they may have life, and that they may have it more abundantly.

God is promising to the tither that He will fight against the enemy for him. God will cover the tither so he will be protected from the curse of the sin of Adam. The ground will produce abundantly and people will see God's prosperity on your life. There are other blessings promised to those who keep the Mosaic covenant which involved keeping the commandments and making sacrifices and offerings regularly. There were three feasts they were to attend and keep. Offerings were given at them.

Levites

The Levites, collected the tithes and offerings. They administered the sacrifices and offerings and they received portions of the offerings for themselves. God gave them the shoulder and breast parts of the meat offerings and a portion of the other offerings. It was their income. Very important is that the Levites and priests also offered up a tithe of all of their income. They gave a tithe from what they were given. It was their worship expression to God. It also kept them pure of pride in believing they were more holy or more worthy than the other tribes because they gave in worship to God the same as all the other tribes.

Numbers 18: 25 The Lord spoke to Moses, saying: 26 You will speak to the Levites, and say to them: When you take from the children of Israel the tithes that I have given you from them for your inheritance, then you will offer up an offering of it to the Lord, even one-tenth of the tithe. 27 And this offering will be counted to you, as though it was the grain of the threshing floor, and as the fullness of the winepress. 28 Thus you also will set apart an offering to the Lord from all the tithes which you receive from the children of Israel. Out of them you will give the offering of the Lord to Aaron the priest. 29 Out of all your gifts you shall present every offering due to the Lord, from all the best of them, the consecrated part of them.

Deuteronomy

The book of Deuteronomy discusses much of the covenant blessings on Israel and Israel's requirements. This portion from Deuteronomy gives the reader the type of blessing God is describing when a person is in covenant with Him. The blessings of God are so awesome that they will be more than what you need and more than you can expect. God will command the blessing on you and your spheres of influence. It includes all places that you go to or dwell in. It includes all the works of your hands or your job or career. It includes your travel. It includes your bank or storage for goods. It includes being set apart by God as a holy people. This includes freedom. People do not have to be addicted to anything. People can be free to live in communion with God. Others will recognize the blessing of God on you. They may not know it is your God, but they will definitely see your prosperity. It includes blessing on children and family. It includes fertility and also of all your animals. It includes a blessing of you and your children wanting to follow God and live a godly life.

Deuteronomy 28: 1 Now it will be, if you will diligently obey the voice of the Lord your God, being careful to do all His commandments which I am commanding you today, then the Lord your God will set you high above all the nations of the earth. 2 And all these blessings will come on you and overtake you if you listen to the voice of the Lord your God.

3 You will be blessed in the city and blessed in the field.

4 Your offspring will be blessed, and the produce of your ground, and the offspring of your livestock, the increase of your herd and the flocks of your sheep.

5 Your basket and your kneading bowl will be blessed.

6 You will be blessed when you come in and blessed when you go out.

7 The Lord will cause your enemies who rise up against you to be defeated before you; they will come out against you one way and flee before you seven ways.

8 The Lord will command the blessing on you in your barns and in all that you set your hand to do, and He will bless you in the land which the Lord your God is giving you.

9 The Lord will establish you as a holy people to Himself, just as He swore to you, if you will keep the commandments of the Lord your God and walk in His ways. 10 All people of the earth shall see that you are called by the name of the Lord, and they shall be afraid of you. 11 The Lord will make you overflow in prosperity, in the offspring of your body, in the offspring of your livestock, and in the produce of your ground, in the land which the Lord swore to your fathers to give you.

12 The Lord will open up to you His good treasure, the heavens, to give the rain to your land in its season and to bless all the work of your hand. You will lend to many nations, but you will not borrow. 13 The Lord will make you the head and not the tail; you will only be above and you will not be beneath, if you listen to the commandments of the Lord your God, which I am commanding you today, to observe and to do them. 14 Also, you shall not turn aside from any of the words which I am commanding you today, to the right hand or to the left, to go after other gods to serve them.

Tithing is not Old Testament only

Tithing did not originate with Moses, although it was recorded as Levitical law as God spoke to Moses. Tithing is first recorded with Abraham gave 1/10 of all he had to Melchizedek. God prospered Abraham abundantly so Abraham recognized and gave to the man of God as the high priest 1/10 of all he had. That is significant. No one in scripture is recorded doing such a thing. It was God's inspiration, because later God spoke it directly to Moses.

Genesis 14: 18 Then Melchizedek king of Salem brought out bread and wine. He was the priest of God Most High. 19 And he blessed him and said,

"Blessed be Abram by God Most High,
    Creator[a] of heaven and earth;
20 and blessed be God Most High,
    who has delivered your enemies into your hand."

Then Abram gave him a tenth of everything.

Jesus did not stop tithing.

Jesus was rebuking Pharisees for their variation of interpreting the law of Moses. He corrected them not because they were tithers but because they were not just or loving. He said they should tithe but also they should have the character of God, of mercy and compassion.

Luke 11: 42 "Woe to you, Pharisees! For you tithe mint and rue and every herb and pass over justice and the love of God. These you ought to have done, without leaving the others undone.

Jesus takes interest in our giving

Jesus watched over the treasury. That is the place people gave alms and offerings and financial gifts. He noticed people putting in much money. He also noticed the widow woman who gave all she had even though it was not much.

Mark 12: 41 Jesus sat opposite the treasury and saw how the people put money into the treasury. Many who were rich put in much.

Jesus teaches the truth of treasure

Jesus did not say that rich or wealthy people could not be saved. What he emphasized is that what we set our heart's affection on determines what we value and treasure. Rich people who are covetous and consider money more important than anything are sinning against God. We should love God and use money – not use God to get money. Also, not only rich people are covetous. There are people who say negative things about wealthy people because they covet their money. They are driven to make foolish comments because they lust after someone else's wealth. The core of Jesus' teaching on money is that we should love God first and care for others. He teaches us to give as unto God.

Matthew 6: 19 "Do not store up for yourselves treasures on earth where moth and rust destroy and where thieves break in and steal. 20 But store up for yourselves treasures in heaven, where neither moth nor rust destroy and where thieves do not break in nor steal, 21 for where your treasure is, there will your heart be also.

John the Baptist taught that those who had more than enough should give to the poor.

Luke 3: 11 John answered, "He who has two tunics, let him give to him who has none. And he who has food, let him do likewise."

Giving

Giving financially is the main aspect of my book but being generous can involve every area of your life. The new testament requirements for a leader included hospitality and showing generosity towards others. My mother had a giving nature. I remember in our bakery, my mother would always give more to those who were not wealthy. I didn't understand about wealth but what I did see is someone buying a loaf of our rye bread and my mother would give them a dozen doughnuts. I remember my nanny had a really large family and she was not wealthy (I did not understand wealth as a child) My mom would often give her doughnuts, pastry, bread and other things we had. She would give clothing.

Titus 1: 7 For an overseer must be blameless, as a steward of God, not self-willed, not easily angered, not given to drunkenness, not violent, not greedy for dishonest gain, 8 but hospitable, a lover of what is good, self-controlled, just, holy, temperate, 9 holding firmly the trustworthy word that is in accordance with the teaching, that he may be able both to exhort with sound doctrine and to convince those who oppose it.

Learning about waste

I was about 3 years old and I delighted in greeting customers in the bakery. One day I remember a serious lesson my mother taught me. I didn't know what wealth was and certainly never knew lack as a child. I would get doughnuts. I didn't understand waste. I remember my mom telling me to choose something and I chose a large chocolate cinnamon bun. I licked it and threw it in the garbage and chose something else. My mother held my arm firmly and spoke to me something that scared me. She told me that I can have whatever I would like but I was never to waste it. She told me there were many people who could not have what we had. She told me many people didn't have money. It was so hard to conceive of because it was beyond what I had experienced. I remember the tone of her voice warning me but also teaching me that we are not to waste anything because some people have nothing.

I began to care about people and animals; it was my start in terms of giving. Once my brother was born I had to share. That was something I did not enjoy. Often, I would not want him to touch my toys or I wanted what he had. It wasn't until we were in mid elementary school that we played together without me wanting his stuff or him wanting mine. Sharing with others is a form of giving. Even after we lost our wealth, my mother stayed generous. We had much less but we did not do without essentials. Often my mother would make extra spaghetti or soup and give a large serving bowl of it to our neighbours who had almost no income at all. I learned it is good to share. If you have more than enough, give to those around you.

Church

At church, many years later, I began tithing. It was really tough sometimes. I would carnally think I could have more money if I didn't give the tithe. When there were bills to pay, I was on my own, I thought about not tithing. More than once, I borrowed the tithe from God, until I got more money and later repaid Him. Within 2 or 3 years, I knew that God was financially prospering me as a tither. It wasn't only the money I made but opportunities would come to me that others didn't get. Special favour was shown to me. There were Christians who taught me about giving. One of my closest friends, like a spiritual parent, would give me bags of clothing. I am not talking about junk. She wore expensive and beautiful clothing. It was always fashionable and we took the same size. She would wear something several times and then give it away. I was a person she gave to. It doesn't sound like much but it was so important.

I only had one skirt my first year of being a Christian. At Teacher's college, when practice teaching, we were expected to dress up. Because of my friend Polly, I had clothing I could wear to church or for my profession.

I was regularly tithing and sometimes giving to missions. Once I had my first job, money wasn't abundant but I had enough for all my needs. I played sports at Church; it was a huge church with all sorts of activities for people of all ages. There was an older man named Ace who would always come to the gym and watch us play volleyball. He also came to watch our baseball games. He was a greeter in the church. I did not know his wife. While he was in my life, he was a widower. I became friendly with him, after several years of seeing him in all the spots I would go to. He helped me find a mechanic. I gave him a ride more than once. I did not know him well but I did know he loved God and he was kind and generous. One of the last occasions I saw him, he spoke to me a scripture. It stuck in me like a blade; I don't mean it was painful; it was profound.

Transformation

Acts 20: 35 In all things I have shown you how, working like this, you must help the weak, remembering the words of the Lord Jesus, how He said, 'It is more blessed to give than to receive.' "

God used that man to prophesy that word about giving to me. I kept thinking of it over and over throughout my life. The reason that giving is more blessed than receiving is because you can never out give God. You can give and give and give; God will always bless you more and more.

That scripture changed me. I started seeing opportunities to give. Also, I got some excellent teaching from Kenneth and Gloria Copeland about giving. It taught me to expect to receive from God as I gave as a seed. As I gave as unto God, God honoured me by prospering me. No one had taught me about giving to other ministries that bless you. I had only known that one church and there were always special missions and charitable things. I did all my giving at my church. The more money I made, the more I gave.

I had to move out of town to get a teaching job. As I did, I got my richest teachings from the Christian television. Kenneth and Gloria Copeland became like family to me because I watched them and always learned something. Often it was a prophetic type of teaching I needed in my life. I started giving to the ministry. I knew that they were feeding me spiritually and I knew I wanted other people to get the same kinds of teaching. They never begged for money. They have never used commercialization tactics. God prompted me to give. I started giving in spurts to this ministry that was really where I was getting my spiritual nourishment. Later, I became a regular partner. I read the scripture myself and it impacted me. I realized they were special to me because I was receiving so much from them. It is a special connection being partners with a ministry.

1 Corinthians 9: 11 If we have sown for you spiritual things, is it a great thing if we shall reap your material things?

GIFT OF GIVING

Mentioned along with other spiritual gifts is the gift of giving. There are people who have a gift from God to give large amounts of money to the gospel. They receive finances, houses, lands, wealth easily. They also give generously. I heard about it from the Copelands. They talked about giving cars, planes etc. I met people who have given their cars as well as their homes to the gospel.

Romans 12: 6 We have diverse gifts according to the grace that is given to us: if prophecy, according to the proportion of faith; 7 if service, in serving; he who teaches, in teaching; 8 he who exhorts, in exhortation; he who gives, with generosity; he who rules, with diligence; he who shows mercy, with cheerfulness.

I became close to people who give these types of extravagant, giving by faith as unto God. I have known of people who have had cars given to them. I believe that should God prompt me to give, I should give. It could be extravagant. God will always bless the person for giving. I am not talking about being foolhardy. I am talking about a gift of giving. God prompts you to give and you give.

I know of preachers that I respect that get a roll of hundred-dollar bills in their pocket and go shopping on purpose. They are financially blessed. They pray and give out hundred-dollar bills to people and let them know Jesus loves them. They tip extravagantly letting them know Jesus cares. They use money to reach people. It is part of their unique spiritual gifting.

I know of other Christians who pay for someone else's (a random person or people) lunch or dinner without them knowing about it. I travel an international border often. There have been occasions where the people in the car ahead of me have paid my toll. I don't know who they are or why they did it. Giving to loved ones is usual. Giving to strangers is uncommon. Extravagant giving is unusual and attracts attention. The person with the gift of giving does it to honour Jesus. The person always points to Jesus.

Giving for match funding

A person with the gift of giving likes to motivate others to give also. Often the person will give a large amount of money with dollar for dollar funding. They promise to give a dollar extra for each person who gives a dollar. It is a motivator to people who usually give to charities that want to see their gift go further by their offer to match funds. Usually, givers do not want their names given. They give with joy and with simplicity.

Giving releases thanksgiving

There is a type of giving that releases thanksgiving in others. Generous giving towards people, often releases special thanksgiving in those people to God. They receive the gift and believe that God provided for them. They rejoice thanking God for His provision. It can impact people spiritually drawing them closer to God.

2 Corinthians 9: 11 So you will be enriched in everything to all bountifulness, which makes us give thanks to God.

12 For the administration of this service not only supplies the need of the saints, but is abundant also through many thanksgivings to God.

A sure way to examine our priorities is to see where we are giving, and to whom we are giving and our motivation for giving. It will reveal the condition of our heart towards God. What we give priority to should be the God and the preaching and teaching of Christ. Other giving should be in areas we care deeply about. If we truly love God, we will give our tithes joyfully thanking God for our provision; we will also want to give to missions and give alms as God prospers us.

Matthew 22: 37 Jesus said to him, " 'You shall love the Lord your God with all your heart, and with all your soul, and with all your mind.'[c] 38 This is the first and great commandment. 39 And the second is like it: 'You shall love your neighbor as yourself.'[d] 40 On these two commandments hang all the Law and the Prophets."

Giving is a sure way to end covetousness. They are opposites. Rather than desire to hoard more finances and resources, the person gives and it mixed with faith produces results not only in the gift amount but a multiplication of it. God causes an anointing of generosity to come up on the person and it releases joy because the person knows he or she is being used by God.

3 ALMS

Chapter 3

The giving of alms is commanded by God in Leviticus. God commanded that any of our crops or trees or fruit bearing plants not be picked clean. They were to leave some extra crops so that those who had nothing could come and gather some for themselves. It was for the widows and orphans and also the strangers.

Leviticus 19: 9 When you reap the harvest of your land, you shall not reap up to the edge of your field, nor shall you gather the gleanings of your harvest. 10 You shall not glean bare your vineyard, nor shall you gather every fallen grape of your vineyard. You shall leave them for the poor and stranger: I am the Lord your God.

Leviticus 23: 22 When you reap the harvest of your land, you shall not reap your field up to the edge, nor shall you gather any gleaning of your harvest. You shall leave them to the poor and to the foreigner: I am the Lord your God.

The Attitude matters

Giving of alms must be done with the right motive. It is not to draw attention to yourself but to give so others may thank God. It is because God has blessed us with more than enough, so we should care for those who have nothing.

Matthew 6: 1 "Be sure that you not do your charitable deeds before men to be seen by them. Otherwise you have no reward from your Father who is in heaven. The people who give so they appear to be generous in the eyes of people get much appreciation and public support. They got their reward. People who give secretly so no one knows about it are giving as unto God himself. A person who gives to help the poor is giving as unto God.

Jesus taught the people not to give for earthly praise but as though you are storing up treasure in heaven. Giving without seeking fame or recognition. It doesn't mean people may not thank you. It does mean the motive of your heart is more important than the actual gift itself.

Matthew 6: 2 "Therefore, when you do your charitable deeds, do not sound a trumpet before you as the hypocrites do in the synagogues and in the streets, that they may be honored by men. Truly I say to you, they have their reward. 3 But when you do your charitable deeds, do not let your left hand know what your right hand is doing, 4 that your charitable deeds may be in secret. And your Father who sees in secret will Himself reward you openly.

Giving the basics

Jesus talks about our giving to those who are needy as a condition of judgement from a heavenly perspective. Both flocks belonged to God: sheep and goats. There was a clear separation though because those on his right hand would inherit eternal life. They met practical needs of people who were needy. Feeding the hungry, clean water to the thirsty, comfort and hospitality towards the stranger, giving of clothing, ministering comfort and healing to the sick and visiting those in prison. These people may seem to be least important in society. It not often you will see their pictures or their biographies. They seem unimportant to average people and especially to the wealthy. They are important to God. Jesus is showing us He values all people. Practical giving of basic necessities is giving as unto God. Jesus says, you give to these people, it is though you are giving directly to Jesus Himself. He is teaching about giving. He is teaching about equality of all people. He is talking about caring for people that can never repay you.

Caring for those who are alone

Caring for the sick is a ministry of mercy. Visiting them, praying with them and giving encouragement to them is as though you are giving to God directly. Sometimes there are people who no one visits. Should you be visiting someone, and there are others who have no visors, a kind word, a prayer, can comfort the person tremendously. It may also lead the person to Jesus Christ. God doesn't hate the sinner. This is a tough thing on religious people. God does not turn away from those in prison. Our visiting them can be a way of drawing them to God., leading them to repent, and turn their lives to God. They may be released from prison because of the changes in their hearts and lives. Sometimes, there are miraculous deliveries for prisoners who turn their lives to Christ. Even if they do not get out of prison, they can be free in their hearts knowing the Saviour and Redeemer. They can share the gospel with others while they are in the prison.

Matthew 25: 31 "When the Son of Man comes in His glory, and all the holy angels with Him, then He will sit on the throne of His glory. 32 Before Him will be gathered all nations, and He will separate them one from another as a shepherd separates his sheep from the goats. 33 He will set the sheep at His right hand, but the goats at the left.

34 "Then the King will say to those at His right hand, 'Come, you blessed of My Father, inherit the kingdom prepared for you since the foundation of the world. 35 For I was hungry and you gave Me food, I was thirsty and you gave Me drink, I was a stranger and you took Me in. 36 I was naked and you clothed Me, I was sick and you visited Me, I was in prison and you came to Me.'

37 "Then the righteous will answer Him, 'Lord, when did we see You hungry and feed You, or thirsty and give You drink? 38 When did we see You a stranger and take You in, or naked and clothe You? 39 And when did we see You sick or in prison and come to You?'

40 "The King will answer, 'Truly I say to you, as you have done it for one of the least of these brothers of Mine, you have done it for Me.'

41 "Then He will say to those at the left hand, 'Depart from Me, you cursed, into the eternal fire, prepared for the devil and his angels. 42 For I was hungry and you gave Me no food, I was thirsty and you gave Me no drink, 43 I was a stranger and you did not take Me in, I was naked and you did not clothe Me, I was sick and in prison and you did not visit Me.'

44 "Then they also will answer Him, 'Lord, when did we see You hungry or thirsty or a stranger or naked or sick or in prison, and did not serve You?'

45 "He will answer, 'Truly I say to you, as you did it not for one of the least of these, you did it not for Me.'

Jesus words should be taught and preached regularly. Giving unto those people, seemingly the most unimportant, is as directly giving to God. God places special blessings on those who care for the poor.

Proverbs 19: 17 He who has pity on the poor lends to the Lord,
    and He will repay what he has given.

Proverbs 28: 27 He who gives to the poor will not lack,
    but he who hides his eyes will have many a curse.

A person who gives to the poor and needy, is directly giving to God. It doesn't mean there might not be scammers who try to get money from you. I live near a large USA city. Often as I shopped and did activities in the core of the city, I was approached by people begging for money. Often I did not have much money of my own, but I would give small denominations –

enough to get a meal. I knew it would not change that person's life completely but it was a way of showing them God cared about them.

The bag lady

One Saturday early, I was heading to my Bible class North of Detroit. It was early. There was still mist on the ground. I saw a woman with a shopping cart with bags in it. I knew it was everything she owned. I felt compelled to stop and give her something. I knew it was the Holy Spirit prompting me with the gift of mercy. I found a way to pull to the side of the road. I got out of my car with money clenched in my hand. As the bag lady who was collecting pop bottles and beer bottles saw me she started walking away as quickly as she could.

God only knows what things had happened to her in her life. She was scared of me. I spoke " Please. Let me give you something." I approached her slowly. She grabbed the money out of my hand and backed away from me. I said God bless you or something like it. I got in the car feeling totally overwhelmed by the experience knowing it was God that moved on my heart to give. I was almost pleased with myself – it wasn't pride but it was a joy that came from knowing that God used me. God spoke to me immediately. He said " I would have taken her home to live with me." O those words got me. I knew that I knew I was nowhere near God was. I tried for one moment to imagine how I possibly could get her over an international border and bring her to my simple home. I was not wealthy. I surely though could care for her basic needs and protect her from thugs. God taught me about giving. I want to be a giver like God wants to be a giver. He thinks of each person as unique, worthy, desirable. He loves each person with so much love that He sent Jesus to die on the cross so that we might have eternal life.

Giving to poor commanded

Jesus made it clear that there would always be people who needed help. If we truly love God, we will truly love people. We will give because it is the right thing.

Matt 26: 11 For ye have the poor always with you; but me ye have not always.

In the book of Acts, we read how the Church cared for each other so that no one went without food or clothing or necessities. A spirit of giving was released upon those who turned to Christ. Those who were wealthy gave of their extra to care for the Christians who had nothing. The Apostles saw that the finances were distributed to those who needed. I am not a Communist. I am not suggesting Communism. I am though stating that in our churches, we should not have any one who attends going without food or clothing. We should care for those in our midst knowing God cherishes them.

Acts 4: 32 All the believers were of one heart and one soul, and no one said that what he possessed was his own. But to them all things were in common. 33 With great power the apostles testified to the resurrection of the Lord Jesus, and great grace was on them all. 34 There was no one among them who lacked, for all those who were owners of land or houses sold them, and brought the income from what was sold, 35 and placed it at the apostles' feet. And it was distributed to each according to his need.

The church should have special care for the widows and orphans. We don't use that language much but there are single, or married, poor and needy people who may need food or clothing. All the churches I have attended have a food bank, a ministry of giving clothing and special givers within the church who see a need and give generously. As churches, we should have some type of system of giving to those who are ours. I know some churches give to anyone who asks. I especially emphasize there are people no different than ourselves except they have not. They attend services; they worship God, but for whatever reasons, they have nothing. We should care for our own. A church is as a family. The first deacons of the church were chosen to care for the widows and their children.

Acts 6: 1 Now in those days, as the disciples were multiplied, there was murmuring among the Hellenists against the Hebrews, because their widows were overlooked in the daily distribution. 2 So the twelve called the multitude of disciples together and said, "It is not reasonable for us to leave the word of God and serve tables. 3 Brothers, look among yourselves for seven men who are known to be full of the Holy Spirit and of wisdom, whom we will appoint over this duty. 4 But we will give ourselves continually to prayer and to the ministry of the word."

The widow's mite

Not only does Jesus care about the treasury and what is given, the heart attitude or motive must be pure and without selfish gain. An example is that Jesus watched people putting much money into the treasury. He saw wealthy people placing large sums of money into it. He notices it but commented on the widow who gave only a mite – a small amount. He commented that she had given more than all of them because she gave all that she had with a pure heart as unto God.

Luke 21: 1 He looked up and saw the rich putting their gifts in the treasury. 2 He also saw a poor widow putting in two mites,[a] 3 and He said, "Truly I tell you, this poor widow has put in more than all of them. 4 For all these out of their abundance have put in their gifts for God. But she out of her poverty has put in all the living she had."

Jesus mercy on the multitudes

The scriptures mention several occasions where Jesus is overcome with compassion on the multitudes who followed him. In this first instance, is compelled to give his prayer request for those who will preach the gospel to the people.

Matthew 9: 36 But when He saw the crowds, He was moved with compassion for them, because they fainted and were scattered, like sheep without a shepherd. 37 Then He said to His disciples, "The harvest truly is plentiful, but the laborers are few. 38 Therefore, pray to the Lord of the harvest, that He will send out laborers into His harvest."

In this instance, his compassion is to feed them. A miracle of multiplication occurs because of it.

Matthew 15: 32 Then Jesus called His disciples to Him and said, "I have compassion on the crowd, because they have remained with Me now for three days and have nothing to eat. I will not send them away hungry, lest they faint on the way."

In this instance, Jesus is compelled to heal them.

Matthew 20: 34 So Jesus had compassion on them and touched their eyes. Immediately their eyes received sight, and they followed Him.

The Apostle James gives a definition of true faith.

Giving to those in need of basic things such as food and clothing is true faith being lived. It is evident with faith and works. Our actions should be as we believe. We should live our faith. We don't do good deeds to score points with God. We give because we worship God and care for people.

James 2: 14 What does it profit, my brothers, if a man says he has faith but has no works? Can faith save him? 15 If a brother or sister is naked and lacking daily food, 16 and one of you says to them, "Depart in peace, be warmed and filled," and yet you give them nothing that the body needs, what does it profit? 17 So faith by itself, if it has no works, is dead.

18 But a man may say, "You have faith and I have works."

Show me your faith without your works, and I will show you my faith by my works.

James further states that caring for the widows and orphans is essential to our faith. Also, he mentions remaining pure in heart and living holy unto God.

James 1: 27 Religion that is pure and undefiled before God, the Father, is this: to visit the fatherless and widows in their affliction and to keep oneself unstained by the world.

It is my hope that in this chapter you understand God's heart for all people. God unconditionally loves and values every person. If we truly love God with all our being, we will care about people and it will be evident in our thoughts, words, deeds and giving. Giving to the poor or the weak is directly giving to God.

4 SOWING A SEED

Chapter 4

Sowing a seed faith, I learned from Oral Roberts. I heard him preach it and knew it was true. Although I heard it, and knew it, I did not immediately apply it until I heard others teaching it and preaching it. The revelation came to me that if I knew it was true, I should start doing it.
I am a gardener so I know that to get tomatoes, I must plant tomatoes; to get corn, I must plant corn; to get radishes, I must plant radishes. The seed has within itself the power to multiply. Preparing the soil is necessary; afterwards planting the seed is essential; if I do not plant the seed, I will not reap from that area. The seed type I plant determines the crop that I will reap. Spiritually, it matters the type of seed I am sowing. The soil matters there are factors that should be prepared by the sower.

Galatians 6: 7 Be not deceived. God is not mocked. For whatever a man sows, that will he also reap. 8 For the one who sows to his own flesh will from the flesh reap corruption, but the one who sows to the Spirit will from the Spirit reap eternal life.

If I sow a seed, and do it with a wrong heart motive, it will not prosper. If I sow a seed that contradicts God's word, it will not prosper. To sow and reap an abundance, I must come into agreement with God's Word. God's Word always produces fruit when it is mixed with faith.

John 6: 63 It is the Spirit who gives life. The flesh profits nothing. The words that I speak to you are spirit and are life.

God's word gives us understanding and revelation of how to live a holy life. God's word is like a light that shows us how to live. It is God's expressed will for us. God's Word not only helps us to live daily, when it is mixed with faith can produce miracles. Faith in God's word combined with patience produces answers to prayers. Promises of God come by faith.

Hebrews 6: 11 We desire that every one of you show the same diligence for the full assurance of hope to the end, 12 so that you may not be lazy, but imitators of those who through faith and patience inherit the promises.

Whatever is not of faith is sin (Romans 14: 23). If we are believing for a promise of God, we should ask God for it in faith and thank God for it. If it is God's Word, it is God's will. If our heart condition is pure, it is

God's delight to give us the thing we ask. It gives God pleasure to give to us.

Luke 12: 32 "Do not be afraid, little flock, for it is your Father's good pleasure to give you the kingdom.

Word of God mixed with faith produces. 30-fold, 60 fold 100 fold

Growth – faith – with word of God as you give – expecting spiritual harvest

Jesus preached the parable of the sower to people who understood sowing and reaping physical seed. Agriculture was a way of life. The sower was sowing seed. Now, this sower wasn't exactly the wisest type of farmer. He sowed some seed on the pathway where it could be trampled underfoot. He sowed some on rocky ground, so the roots couldn't grow deeply. He planted where there were thorns and weeds that choked the good plant. Finally, he sowed some in good soil.

I am not a farmer but a gardener. They are similar but not exactly the same. The farmer plants enough so he or she can make a living. I plant only for my own use and to give family and friends. My dad was raised on a farm in the prairies. I had opportunity to see the land there. It was so long I could not see the end of the area. In every direction I searched, I could not see the end of the land. It was a huge plot of land. They made their living by agriculture. They turned the soil not with shovels but by a huge machine. They reaped their harvest not with their hands but with machines. Jesus gives the parable of the sower.

Mark 4: 1 Again He began to teach by the seaside. A large crowd was gathered before Him, so that He entered a boat and sat in it on the sea. And the whole crowd was by the sea on the land. 2 He taught them many things in parables and said to them in His teaching: 3 "Listen! And take note: A sower went out to sow. 4 As he sowed, some seed fell beside the path, and the birds of the air came and devoured it. 5 Some seed fell on rocky ground, where it did not have much soil, and soon it sprang up because it did not have deep soil. 6 But when the sun rose, it was scorched. And because it had no root, it withered away. 7 Other seed fell among thorns, and the thorns grew up and choked it, and it yielded no grain. 8 And other seed fell on good ground, and it yielded grain that sprang up and increased by thirty, sixty, or a hundred times as much."

9 Then He said to them, "He who has ears to hear, let him hear."

Soil condition must be proper for the seed to grow properly. First it is important to dig to loosen the soil; take out any weeds; create planting valley rows. Next plant the seed you want to grow. Finally, cover the seed rows with soil. Farmers use irrigation systems. My dad`s farm relied on rain. I water my plants with a hose. The seed is planted into good soil. I have seen good soil. Rich fertile black soil that will produce anything. I have also had the task of having hard clay soil that had to be fertilized and mulched and cared for until it became fertile soil. If we plant in any other type of soil than rich fertile soil, it is foolish. Therefore for my analogy, our hearts must be pure. There cannot be any wrong motive of any kind. If we are to plant seed in faith, the soil is our hearts. I don`t mean the physical organ. I mean the inner most self, the spirit.

I plant the Word of God in my life daily. I don`t just mean reading the word of God although it is certainly excellent. Praying God`s word is a way of directly planting the Word into our hearts. We should sow and keep sowing the Word of God into our hearts daily – even if there is no immediate need. What happens as we pray the word of God is that is takes root in our spirit. The Word of God – the Logos – God`s written word is mixed with our faith as we pray it and becomes RHEMA word or revealed or quickened word to us.

Just as a person requires food, our spirits requires spiritual nourishment from God`s Word. If a need arises, the Holy Spirit quickens God`s Word within us and we will pray it, believe it and confess it and it will manifest the answer to the need. As sure as I plant tomatoes and get tomatoes, I plant God`s Word and reap from God`s Word. Some people wait until they have an important need before planting God`s Word in their hearts. That is not wise. The more of God`s Word that we plant, the more of God`s Word the Holy Spirit will quicken and it will become as the answer to the situation. It would be like fasting from food, until you are dying of malnutrition. That would be foolish. Daily we require God`s Word. Daily we get value by sowing God`s Word into our lives. There is immediate joy as well as a harvest from the seed. I rejoice as I pray God`s word over my life. As I see it producing fruit I rejoice. It is like my gardening. I rejoice at the first tomatoes or cucumbers or whatever. There is a joy in reaping.

Jesus explains the parable in the following scriptures.

What is important is that soil condition matters.

Mark 4: 13 Then He said to them, "Do you not understand this parable? How then will you understand all the parables? 14 The sower sows the word. 15 These are those beside the path, where the word is sown. But when they hear, Satan comes immediately and takes away the word which is sown in their hearts. 16 Others, likewise, are seed sown on rocky ground, who, when they hear the word, immediately receive it with gladness, 17 but have no root in themselves, and so endure for a time. Afterward, when affliction or persecution rises for the word's sake, immediately they fall away. 18 And others are seed sown among thorns, the ones who hear the word. 19 But the cares of this world, and the deceitfulness of riches, and the desires for other things entering in choke the word, and it proves unfruitful. 20 Still others are seed sown on good ground, those who hear the word, and receive it, and bear fruit: thirty, sixty, or a hundred times as much."

These scriptures can be discussed for other purposes but for the purpose of my book, I want to emphasize soil condition matters. Heart condition matters. Preparing our heart means that we are praying, worshipping, valuing God and keeping the commandments. God's Word can grow fully in such a soil condition. I am only going to discuss the good soil. It produces 30, 60 and 100 fold. What it literally means is that if I plant a seed of corn, a corn plant will grow. It will have more than one ear of corn on it in maturity. It is possible for a seed to grow into a plant that has more than 100 kernels of corn on it. It should produce 100-fold of the soil is good condition and the seed is good. Faith determines the harvest often.

I would explain it as what you are asking from God and expecting God to supply determines what you will receive. Faith is the key aspect. If I pray for a new bicycle, believing in faith for it, God will supply a new bicycle. It doesn't mean I won't have to work for it. It doesn't mean that I shouldn't keep thanking Him for it until it manifests. It is not wrong to ask God for physical things that we can use on earth. God tells us to ask of Him. Some people believe the lie that God doesn't want us to have physical things. It is ridiculous because God gave us the ability to create and invent these things; they are for our use.

If I could reap a 100-fold on every word of God that I sow to my life, I would be prosperous in every area of my life. I sow the Word of God because it is God's Word, His will, His desires for us. I sow in faith, believing that God will multiply the seed sown so that I can apply the Word of God to every aspect of my existence. The Holy Spirit quickens the Word to me and as I come into agreement with God`s Word, I see the fruit of my seed. God supplies all my needs, not just enough but more than enough. God blesses us with more than enough so we can continue to sow and so we can continue to give to others.

Should a special need occur, such as a physical thing, of if there is a need for healing, faith mixed with the word of God can manifest.

As discussed, tithing is a commandment. As we give our tithes, we should thank God for what He has done for us but also name a seed that we are sowing into. For instance, as I sow the finances into the kingdom of God, I could pray for God`s revelation, or I could pray for God`s protection, or I could pray for financial prosperity. Giving, without sowing (believing God for something as you give) is good; God will bless you; O you could reap so much more should you sow it in faith believing for something specific. Receive the harvest from God by thanking Him and praising Him.

Special gifts of seed

There was a period in my life where I could not get a job. It was long. There were no teaching jobs. I applied to many places. I did other types of work such as physical labour, painting, and odd jobs. I studied to be a teacher; I desired to teach so strongly, it is hard to express; I knew God created me to teach. It is a part of what I love to do. I developed the gift by getting an education and I wanted the chance to do it. I often watched Christian television so that I could get God`s Word on the inside of me to encourage me, prepare my heart and learn. One preacher was talking about seed faith. I knew it or I thought I knew it, but I had not been doing it. What little income I had, I gave a tithe, but I wasn`t planting anything. What occurred is I realized is that if I named my seed in faith, God would honour my faith. Those words jumped out at me. In faith naming the seed to reap the harvest. The man gave testimony of how God miraculously supplied for him after sowing a special offering to God as an act of faith. Sowing a significant amount, not just the tithe but a special offering as a token to God that you in faith are believing for a harvest.

I am not saying you give to get. That would be a wrong motive. You give as an act of faith; expecting that God will supply. Notice I am choosing the words because heart motive matters. The man explained how much he gave. It was all he owned. He gave it all. Supernaturally, God supplied for him and began to bless him in a new direction. The preacher said something that impacted me much. To get something you have never had before, you must do something you have never done before. I knew it was true. It made sense. If I wanted something new, I had to do something new. I did not have the amount of money the preacher said he gave. He did not tell people how much money to give. He was only giving an example. I knew that I did not have that much money. It was not possible. What I did though is in my heart I spoke to God and said that if he supplied for me that amount I would sow it as a seed. I gave an offering of what I could do financially. It wasn.t immediate. I gave a token offering on the total I felt to give promising God the rest if He would supply it.

As a seed must be buried with earth, and watered and receive sunshine, so must you sow your seed spiritually, believing and praising God for the answer and thanking God for supplying it before you literally see the results. I have been a gardener since I was a child. My mother taught me how to plant flowers. I enjoyed it. In my teens I started my own garden. Later, I kept doing it. It brought joy to me to plant things that made our property appear beautiful. At one point, as a teen, I planted seed one week. Within a week I expected to see sprouts on the top of the ground. There were none. I literally turned over a part of the soil to see if there were any sprouts. The seed had sprouted but it wasn't ready. Gardiners do not do that foolish thing. They realize, they plant and water but God does the growing (1 Corinthians 3: 6).

Within 6 months of my special gift and prayer to God, I was given a temporary job opportunity as a teacher. It wasn.t permanent, but it was a job teaching! I thanked God so much. Also, when the money came in, I planted a seed, the amount I had promised God I would give. I kept my promise. Something happened though. I had never given that much money before. I changed on the inside. I told God I wanted to give that much each year or more. Something was released in me as I gave that first large amount. I started seeing how important it is to give generously to the gospel because the non-Christians are not going to fund it. For Apostles, Prophets, Evangelists, Teachers, and Pastors to minister the gospel as a living, some partners had to join with them financially. I choose to be partners with other ministries that were doing what I wanted to do – bring God's word to all kinds of people all over the world, help people that no one was helping, care for widows and orphans.

Partnership

Giving as a partner to a ministry that preaches Christ, feeds the hungry, cares for the poor or the weak, makes us a partner with that ministry. What partnership means is that a measure of the anointing that is on that ministry comes on your life. You care about them. You become involved with their giving and events. You attend partner gatherings and crusades and special events. You meet other people like yourself. You share the same values. You share in the blessings of that ministry. As King David was fighting, some of the men stayed a place to replenish themselves. They guarded the stuff. They were not in the battle the others were in. Some people who had won the battle said the others could not have any share in it because they did not own it. King David corrected them. He said those who stayed were one with them and they would share the treasure equally.

1 Samuel 30: 23 Then David said, "You will not do so, my brothers, with what the Lord has given us, for He has preserved us, and has delivered into our hand the raiding party that came against us. 24 And who will listen to you in this matter? Indeed as the share is of the one going down to battle, so will be the share of the one staying with the equipment. They will share equally." 25 So it was so from that day forward, that he set it as a statute and an ordinance for Israel to this day.

As I give financially, prayerfully to a ministry, I reap some of the reward. Some of it is spiritual. Truly those ministries feed me spiritually. Truly I get excited about their missionary trips and their giving to the poor etc. God honours my giving and my faith, that I become a partaker of the blessings of winning souls, helping people, preaching the gospel. God sees our giving and our heart motive for giving. God will bless those who give to the gospel.

Mark 9: 41 Truly I say to you, whoever gives you a cup of water to drink in My name, because you belong to Christ, will not lose his reward.

Keeping your heart right

As you sow, you will reap. Our motive for giving though should be faith in God. We should not give to get. The difference is totally completely real. Sowing in faith and receiving is essential to receiving from God. Giving to get is a heart motive much like playing the lottery. You hope you get lucky. That is not a right motive for giving to God. There is no faith in it and it is covetousness. Seeking God first is the essential aspect. Faith towards God is what plants your seed that grows.

Matthew 6: 33 But seek first the kingdom of God and His righteousness, and all these things shall be given to you.

Keep your eyes on the prize

Our giving and receiving should be with our heart fixed on Jesus. It is God's mercy towards us and his joy to give to us and provide for us. The prize is not what we pray for. Jesus is our prize. He is our champion, our Saviour, redeemer, provider.

Hebrews 12: 2 Let us look to Jesus, the author and finisher of our faith, who for the joy that was set before Him endured the cross, despising the shame, and is seated at the right hand of the throne of God.

High calling

The high calling is not an achievement; it is living your life wholly unto God honouring God in all you do. Keeping it as a main priority of your life will help you to keep your heart right.

Philippians 3: 14 I press toward the goal to the prize of the high calling of God in Christ Jesus.

Treasures in heaven – spiritual seed

Jesus spoke the following as a caution that we should be caring about storing up treasure in heaven. Granaries are used to store bulk grain. I see them. They are huge structures that literally store grain. As a youth, I had a closet so small, I could barely enter it. I put all sorts of sports equipment and clothing in there. It did not look very organized. Later, I moved into a home; as I started working, I acquired things such as sports equipment, radios, skis. I stored the stuff in my basement. The longer a person lives, he or she will acquire stuff. Storage seems to be of prime essence. Jesus knew this truth for all people. That is why he used the analogy to store up in heaven. What we store in heaven is by faith. It is through prayer, righteous deeds, and faith confessions. We sow spiritually but it is real substance and real treasure. It is spiritual though. We will inherit what we sow on earth. If we live our lives unto God, we will reap a heavenly reward. If we live selfishly only for our own selves, we will reap what we sow, with little or no treasure in heaven.

Matthew 6: 19 "Do not store up for yourselves treasures on earth where moth and rust destroy and where thieves break in and steal. 20 But store up for yourselves treasures in heaven, where neither moth nor rust destroy and where thieves do not break in nor steal, 21 for where your treasure is, there will your heart be also.

Mustard seed faith

Faith as small as a mustard seed is so mighty that it can move a mountain. Faith is a spiritual substance that is necessary in our dealings with God. If we plant our seed with faith, it has within it the potential to make itself come to pass. The seed has the life potential in it. People have found seeds that were in Egyptian tombs. They planted some. It was thousands of years old but it sprouted and grew. The seed is mighty; the seed with faith is miraculous.

Matthew 17: 20 Jesus said to them, "Because of your unbelief. For truly I say to you, if you have faith as a grain of mustard seed, you will say to this mountain, 'Move from here to there,' and it will move. And nothing will be impossible for you. 21 But this kind does not go out except by prayer and fasting."

Mustard seed tree

A tiny seed, such as a mustard seed can grow into a huge tree. There is potential beyond what appears once you plant a seed. Often people plant trees too near their home because they do not estimate the size of the full grown tree. The seed you sow and that is released by faith to grow can not only help you but also those around you. Your blessings can be not only for you but for those around you.

Matthew 13: 31 He told them another parable, saying, "The kingdom of heaven is like a grain of mustard seed which a man took and sowed in his field. 32 This indeed is the least of all seeds, but when it has grown, it is the greatest among herbs and is a tree, so that the birds of the air come and lodge in its branches."

Growth

What is important is to realize that planting and reaping are seasons. I live in a part of Canada that experiences all seasons. I know that I should not plant my garden until the frost is done. If I start planting things too early, the seed could be frozen. I also know that once the harvest begins, it is important to start reaping. New ripe fruit or vegetables are ready and should be gathered. There is a process sowing spiritual seed also. You plant; you water by faith – praying thanking God for it, praising God for it and finally receiving it.

Mark 4: 28 For the earth bears fruit by itself: first the blade, then the head, then the full seed in the head. 29 But when the grain is ripe, immediately he applies the sickle because the harvest has come."

Sow as unto God – name your seed

If we speak it in faith and pray it in faith, God will honour our faith. The words of our mouth and what we believe is so important it can influence our world. It can affect our future. That is why it is essential to align with God's Word and to pray God's word and to keep sowing it in our hearts so that it might become full grown in our lives. We should believe what God says in His word. We should align our lives with God's Word. Faith with God's word will produce abundant results.

Mark 11: 22 Jesus answered them, "Have faith in God. 23 For truly I say to you, whoever says to this mountain, 'Be removed and be thrown into the sea,' and does not doubt in his heart, but believes that what he says will come to pass, he will have whatever he says. 24 Therefore I say to you, whatever things you ask when you pray, believe that you will receive them, and you will have them

Give and keep giving

This passage of Scripture was quickened to me as I heard Kenneth Copeland preach it. To give and keep on giving. Should you give, surely you shall receive. Keep giving in every season. It explains that some people will not sow because of the weather. If you can't sow in the yard, start your seed in the house. If you sow and keep sowing you will reap not one harvest but many. For instance, tomatoes usually ripen in July. Lettuce and carrots ripen quicker. They can also be replanted so that I could plant and reap from those plantings several times during a growing season. To compare it to giving, give and diversify your giving. Pray in faith believing for your harvest. You will reap the benefits over a duration not just all at once.

Ecclesiastes 11: 1Cast thy bread upon the waters: for thou shalt find it after many days.
2Give a portion to seven, and also to eight; for thou knowest not what evil shall be upon the earth.
3If the clouds be full of rain, they empty themselves upon the earth: and if the tree fall toward the south, or toward the north, in the place where the tree falleth, there it shall be.
4He that observeth the wind shall not sow; and he that regardeth the

clouds shall not reap.

5As thou knowest not what is the way of the spirit, nor how the bones do grow in the womb of her that is with child: even so thou knowest not the works of God who maketh all.

6In the morning sow thy seed, and in the evening withhold not thine hand: for thou knowest not whether shall prosper, either this or that, or whether they both shall be alike good.

Sowing by faith is the main key. Prayer and faith with the word of God brings a blessing to the believer.

5 THANKSGIVING OFFERING
Chapter 5

Thanksgiving offerings are literally thanksgiving offerings. They are voluntary. The person who gives them either has a special reason to give extra to God or feels a prompting to give to a Church or ministry above and beyond other giving. It is beyond the tithe. The origin is Leviticus. There are several people in scripture who have given extravagantly towards God with this type of offering.

The origin is the giver in an expression of thanks. Moses was commanded to give the procedure to Aaron and the priests so that people would have a consistent way of giving. There is no new testament equivalent in terms of giving a procedure. It had to be eaten the same day it was offered.

Leviticus 7: 11And this is the law of the sacrifice of peace offerings, which he shall offer unto the LORD.
12If he offer it for a thanksgiving, then he shall offer with the sacrifice of thanksgiving unleavened cakes mingled with oil, and unleavened wafers anointed with oil, and cakes mingled with oil, of fine flour, fried.
13Besides the cakes, he shall offer for his offering leavened bread with the sacrifice of thanksgiving of his peace offerings.
14And of it he shall offer one out of the whole oblation for an heave offering unto the LORD, and it shall be the priest's that sprinkleth the blood of the peace offerings.
15And the flesh of the sacrifice of his peace offerings for thanksgiving shall be eaten the same day that it is offered; he shall not leave any of it until the morning.
Leviticus 22: 29 When you offer a sacrifice of thanksgiving to the Lord, offer it so that it may be accepted. 30 On the same day it shall be eaten. You shall leave none of it until the next day: I am the Lord.

Motive is to honour God

The person who desires to give a thanksgiving offering may give money, possessions etc. Sometimes it is known as lavish giving. The people who give may be giving more than people would consider normal.

Sometimes lavish

King David and the ark of the covenant -giving

King David is an excellent example who gave extravagantly with thanksgiving. Not only did he give to God directly but also to all the people who came as they brought the ark of the covenant home to Jerusalem. At every 6 paces, King David offered up a sacrifice. There were many steps on their approach to Jerusalem. What it was is an offering to God most extravagant with gratitude that the ark of the covenant, the commandments, Aaron's rod that budded and some manna inside along with God's Holy Presence returning to Jerusalem the capital of Israel. David personally showed his thanksgiving by dancing with all his might in the procession. He gave thanks using his body, soul and spirit as well as by offering sacrifices. It was like a welcoming parade of thanksgiving to God.

2 Samuel 6: 12 When it was reported to King David, "The Lord has blessed Obed-Edom and everything that belongs to him, for the sake of the ark of God," David went and brought up the ark of God from the house of Obed-Edom to the City of David with rejoicing. 13 When those who were carrying the ark of the Lord had taken six steps, David would sacrifice an ox and a fattened steer. 14 David danced before the Lord with all of his might, and he wore a linen ephod. 15 So David and the whole house of Israel escorted the ark of the Lord with shouting and the sound of the horn.

David erected a tabernacle for the ark of the covenant to dwell in. Afterwards, King David offered burnt offerings and peace offerings (also known as thanksgiving offerings). His extravagance of celebration also included giving to all the people who attended the celebration. He gave to God and also gave to people: bread, a date cake, a raisin cake. What occurred is that all of Israel celebrated the return of the ark of the LORD. They were partakers in the feast because David lavishly gave them presents and made of it a huge celebration.

2 Samuel 6: 17 They brought the ark of the Lord and set it in its place inside the tent that David had erected for it. Then David offered burnt offerings and peace offerings before the Lord. 18 When David had finished offering the burnt offerings and peace offerings, he blessed the people before the Lord of Hosts. 19 He distributed to all of the people, the entire multitude of Israel, both men and women, one bread cake, one date cake, and one raisin cake to each one. Then all of the people left, each to his house.

While David lived worshipping God, with the Tabernacle of God in their midst, they enjoyed many years of peace and prosperity.

Solomon built the first Temple of God

Later Solomon dedicates a Temple built to Jehovah where the ark of the covenant would be. There is a tremendous celebration as Israel gathered to see the dedication of the Temple.

2 Chronicles 6: 3 Then the king turned his face around, and he blessed the entire assembly of Israel while all the assembly of Israel was standing before him. 4 And he said:

"Blessed be the Lord God of Israel who spoke with David my father and fulfilled His promise saying, 5 'Since the day that I brought out My people from the land of Egypt, I did not choose any city from among the tribes of Israel to build a house for My name to dwell there, nor did I select a man to be the leader over My people Israel; 6 but I have chosen Jerusalem for My name to dwell there, and I have selected David to be over My people Israel.'

7 "And it was in the heart of David my father to build a house for the name of the Lord God of Israel. 8 But the Lord said to David my father, 'Whereas it was in your heart to build a house for My name, you did well because of what was in your heart; 9 only you will not be the one to build the house. For your son, who will be born to you, he will build a house for My name.'

10 "The Lord has fulfilled the word that He spoke. For I have risen up in the place of David my father and sit on the throne of Israel, as the Lord spoke, and I will build the house for the name of the Lord God of Israel. 11 And there I have set the ark, in which is the covenant of the Lord that He made with the children of Israel."

Solomon's giving

He explains that God instructed David how to build the temple in detail, but Solomon was to build the temple. Solomon invested much effort and David had acquired all of the equipment and materials so that it could be used in the building of the Temple. Solomon offered extravagant numbers of animals for the offerings. He did it to honour God. His lavish giving was his own desire to honour God. 22 thousand oxen and 120 thousand sheep – there was no processing plant there. All of the offerings were slain and roasted and offered as prescribed by the Levitical law.

2 Chronicles 7: 4 Then the king and all the people were making sacrifices before the Lord. 5 King Solomon sacrificed twenty-two thousand oxen and one hundred and twenty thousand sheep. So the king and all the people dedicated the house of God. 6 The priests stood at their positions, with the Levites and all their instruments of music for the Lord that King David had made to praise the Lord—for His mercy endures forever—when David gave praise by their ministry, and the priests sounded trumpets opposite the Levites, and all Israel stood.

7 And Solomon consecrated the middle of the court that was in front of the house of the Lord because there he made burnt offerings and the fat of peace offerings (because the bronze altar that Solomon made was surely not able to contain the burnt offerings, grain offerings, and fat offerings).

The Temple

Afterwards, Solomon proclaimed a huge month-long festival of celebration. He got all of Israel to gather and celebrate the dedication of the Temple. Please see the importance of it. Moses had been instructed to build the ark. God's Holy presence filled the ark. David had brought the ark of the covenant home to Jerusalem after it had been taken by the enemy. David built a Tabernacle, a temporary resting place for the ark. Solomon built the first Temple. All of Israel could go offer sacrifices to God as God instructed Moses. They could pray there. They could about God there. It was a place consecrated for God's glory. It was a place people knew God's presence was in. It wasn't like today where people could pray anywhere because God's Holy Spirit lives within us. It was a physical place people could go to know that God's presence was there.

2 Chronicles 7: 8 And at the appointed time, Solomon made a feast for seven days, and all Israel—as a very great assembly—was with him, from the entrance of Lebo Hamath in the north to the Brook of Egypt in the south. 9 Then on the eighth day they made a solemn assembly because they had made a consecration of the altar for seven days and then the feast for seven days more. 10 Then on the twenty-third day of the seventh month Solomon sent the people away to their homes. They were joyful and good of heart because of what the Lord had done for David, Solomon, and His people Israel.

Josiah giving

Later, in history after many wicked kings, came Josiah a good king.

After the book of the law had been found, and the temple had been repaired, Josiah read the words of God to the people. He made covenant that Israel would follow God. His thanksgiving is celebrated by the re-establishing God's temple as a place of worship. He also re-established the Passover celebration.

2 Kings 23: 1 Then the king sent them away and they gathered all the elders of Judah and Jerusalem to him. 2 The king went up to the house of the Lord, and all the men of Judah and all the inhabitants of Jerusalem with him, the priests, the prophets, and all the people, both small and great. He read in their hearing all the words of the Book of the Covenant that was found in the house of the Lord. 3 The king stood by a pillar and made a covenant before the Lord to follow the Lord, to keep His commandments, His testimonies, and His statutes with all his heart and all his soul, to perform the words of this covenant that were written in this book. All the people agreed with the covenant.

The Model of The Temple

The model of the Temple style of worship can be seen in Psalm 100. Verse 4 speaks of coming into the gates with thanksgiving. That would have been the literal outer court, the place of thanksgiving offerings and other types of offerings being made to God.

Next praise and worship was offered in the Holy place. The priests offered incense.

The most Holy place, no one but the high priest could enter once a year. He had to have a chord with bells tied around his ankle because if the bells stopped ringing, it meant the high priest had unconfessed sinned and died there. No people had access into the most Holy place.

Psalm 100
1Make a joyful noise unto the LORD, all ye lands.
2Serve the LORD with gladness: come before his presence with singing.
3Know ye that the LORD he is God: it is he that hath made us, and not we ourselves; we are his people, and the sheep of his pasture.
4Enter into his gates with thanksgiving, and into his courts with praise: be thankful unto him, and bless his name.
5For the LORD is good; his mercy is everlasting; and his truth endureth to all generations.

The most Holy place was opened to us through Jesus Christ who died as the lamb of God for our sins. He rose from the dead and ascended into heaven and sent us the Holy Spirit. We no longer need to go to a place. The Holy of Holies is now made available to us by the sacrifice of Jesus Christ. God lives within us; we have become a dwelling place for the Spirit of God. We are as the ark of the covenant. God's Holy presence lives in us. In the Old Testament, people had to sacrifice animals to cover over their sin. Because Jesus died on the cross, His blood was sprinkled on the mercy seat in Heaven. His blood purchased our freedom so that we could have direct access to God. We can commune with God throughout the day; God is always with us. His Holy Spirit lives inside of us.

2 Corinthians 4: 7 But we have this treasure in earthen vessels, the excellency of the power being from God and not from ourselves.
Christians have direct access to God. We can directly praise God or pray.

Intimacy with God

I highly recommend the progression of offering thanksgiving, offering thanks, offering praise, worshipping and offering petition or supplication. That is the model of the Tabernacle of Moses, The Tabernacle of David, The Temple of God. That is a model that God taught us, entering in to the most Holy. It is a progressive pressing into God's Holy presence. It comes by an expression of human will. I decide to thank God and praise God. I worship God. I offer prayers and petitions. I thank God. Always give as an expression of worship, not as a duty or something that is not important.

Hebrews 4: 16 Let us then come with confidence to the throne of grace, that we may obtain mercy and find grace to help in time of need.

Present Day Thanksgiving Offerings

Thanksgiving offerings today can include worshipping God with all your being, dancing, giving financially to the gospel, giving of gifts to people because of God and honouring God in some way, huge parties or feasts where we honour God and celebrate with people such as the Messianic celebration of Passover, or the celebration of Christmas or Easter or nights to honour Israel. It can include dinner, speeches, reading God's word and giving of gifts.

6 FREE WILL OFFERING

Chapter 6

Free will offerings are special offerings given to God. They may be in response to a call from a pastor or elder for materials. For instance, God gave Moses specific instruction on gathering materials for the Tabernacle in the wilderness. It was to be the place where the ark of the covenant was stored. Many materials were required. Precious animal skins and wood and spices and gold and silver were required to build the tabernacle to complete the plans according to God's instructions. God instructed Moses to gather the materials and the skilled craftsmen to do the work of the tabernacle, the ark of the covenant and all that would become part of Israel's way of worshipping God for the next generation. Moses made it clear. It was not a command, but those of a "willing heart" were to bring their offerings to God. Skilled craftspeople came to volunteer to do fashion the items of worship such as the lampstand and the sockets and garments for the priests. God the origin of freewill offerings

What is clear is that God is the origin of Judaism not man. God instructed them to build things according to God's words to Moses. Moses made the call to the people of Israel as God had instructed him. Only those who were willing to give had to give. The people of Israel realized that God's Holy presence was going to be in the midst of them and they gave willingly of their skills and of their goods. They realized they were on the start of a new relationship with God. Never before had there been a place especially made for God's presence in their midst. They desired God's presence. The building of the Tabernacle was a sign of the living covenant of God with Israel.

Exodus 35: 4 Moses said to all the congregation of the children of Israel: This is the thing which the Lord commanded, saying: 5 Take from among you an offering to the Lord. Whoever is of a willing heart, let him bring it as an offering to the Lord: gold, silver, and bronze, 6 and blue, purple, and scarlet, fine linen, goats' hair, 7 rams' skins dyed red, and porpoise skins, and acacia wood, 8 oil for the light, and spices for anointing oil, and for the fragrant incense, 9 onyx stones, and gemstones to be set for the ephod and for the breastplate.
10 Every skilled craftsman among you shall come and make all that the Lord has commanded: 11 the tabernacle with its tent and its covering, its

hooks and its boards, its bars, its pillars, and its sockets; 12 the ark with its poles, the mercy seat, and the veil that conceals it; 13 the table with its poles, and all its utensils, and the showbread; 14 the lampstand also for the light and its utensils and its lamps, and the oil for the light; 15 and the incense altar with its poles, and the anointing oil and the fragrant incense, and the hanging for the door at the entrance of the tabernacle; 16 the altar of burnt offering with its bronze grating, its poles, and all its utensils, the basin and its stand; 17 the hangings of the court, its pillars and their sockets, and the curtain for the gate of the court; 18 the pegs of the tabernacle and the pegs of the court and their cords; 19 the woven garments for serving in the holy place, the holy garments for Aaron the priest and the garments of his sons, to minister as priests.

Response in giving

The response of the people was tremendous. People came and brought their jewelry and any spoils of Egypt they had. People brought the expensive animal skins and fabric. Men and women responded so that all the requirements were brought in by the people. The spirit of giving was upon the people so strong that they gave more than what was needed. Suddenly, the huge task of building the specific expensive tabernacle of God was complete. The people gave willingly of themselves.

Exodus 35: 20 Then all the congregation of the children of Israel departed from the presence of Moses. 21 Everyone whose heart stirred him and everyone whose spirit was willing came and brought the Lord's offering for the work of the tent of meeting and for all its service and for the holy garments. 22 They came, both men and women, as many as had willing hearts, and brought brooches, earrings, rings and bracelets, all kinds of gold jewelry, and everyone that offered an offering of gold to the Lord. 23 Everyone who had blue, purple, and scarlet, and fine linen, and goats' hair, and red skins of rams, and porpoise skins, brought them. 24 Everyone who was making a contribution of silver and bronze brought the Lord's offering, and everyone who had acacia wood for any work of the service brought it. 25 All the women that were skilled spun with their hands and brought what they had spun, both of blue, purple, and scarlet, and of fine linen. 26 All the women whose hearts stirred them to action and were skilled spun goats' hair. 27 The leaders brought onyx stones and gemstones to be set for the ephod and for the breastplate, 28 and spice and oil for the light, and for the anointing oil, and for the fragrant incense. 29 The children of Israel brought a willing offering to the Lord, every man and woman whose heart was willing to bring material for all the work which the Lord had commanded through Moses to be made.

The next passage of scripture explains that the people brought more than enough materials and the people who were using it told Moses to stop the people from giving because they had met their goal. Moses spoke to the people of Israel telling them to stop giving.

Exodus 36: Moses called Bezalel and Oholiab and every skilled person in whom the Lord had put wisdom, everyone whose heart stirred him to come to the work to do it. 3 They received from Moses all the offerings which the children of Israel had brought to do the work of the service of the sanctuary, and they continued to bring to him freewill offerings every morning. 4 And all the skilled men who were doing all the work of the sanctuary came from the work they were doing, 5 and they said to Moses, "The people are bringing much more than is needed for the service of the work which the Lord commanded us to do."
6 So Moses issued a command, and they circulated a proclamation throughout the camp, saying, "Let no man or woman do any more work for the offering of the sanctuary." So the people were restrained from bringing any more. 7 For the material they had was sufficient for all the work and more than enough to do it.

20 century application

It is amazing that people could be moved on to do such a thing – give whatever they have so that something of God can be built or established. I have been part a church in a building program. The task of building a church large enough seemed way beyond our budget. There was a plot of ground we purchased in an area North of the present church. The cost of building what we wanted was more than we could imagine.

A preacher visited our church and preached the scripture above. She taught on giving a willing offering to God for the building of the new church that would be double in size. Wealthy people could give generously but the average people, couldn't give much more than they were. She preached on giving a freewill offering of your talents and skills. Rather than be the literal craftspeople, someone could take a part time job and use the money from it for the building of the church. Hairdressers could donate one day a week finances toward the church building.

We hosted auctions as fundraisers with all the people either donating of purchasing new items. People donated free services such as car washes, dinners, tax services etc. The people of the church responded with a willing heart. It was temporary but many sacrificed their time, their treasures and their talents for finances for the church to be built. It took several years. There were bake sales, special luncheons, as well as fancy fund raiser dinners. There was a willing spirit of giving in the people. That church had been in that place for almost 50 years. The move to a new church, much larger, was exciting. We loved our old place but there wasn't enough room for all the people. We had two Sunday services because we could not all fit in the building. We also had an overflow chapel room because sometimes on Sunday night, the church was completely filled' people would watch and listen to the service in the overflow chapel.

There were kinds of giving that are special as well. Some of the tradespeople who worked on the church (not all of them were Christians) became Christians and joined our church. Others offered reduced prices for their services when they saw we were building a place of worship skilled craftsmen donated talents such as carving wood and placing marble tiling. Beautiful stained glass windows were installed as well as other ordinary windows. Nothing was done without excellence. I would describe my living through those years as being a part of something bigger than myself knowing that it would leave a legacy for God.

It is a spirit of giving

In a different church, also in a building renovating project I have known people who took out mortgages on their homes to donate all the money to the building of our new Church. We turned an old factory that was bare cement and turned it into a beautiful sanctuary with classrooms and an upper level of classrooms and extra chapel so that we could allow other churches to come stay with us until they could afford a larger building. We did much of the construction ourselves because the pastors were knowledgeable about these things and members of our congregation were skilled tradesmen. I gave what I could financially which wasn't much at that point in my life. I gave of my efforts.

For several months, I helped pour cement, lay bricks, place drywall and clean the church so afterwards we could meet in the building for worship. We started with bare cement and it was cold. Within a year the church was mostly complete. There were other churches who became a part of our building, helping to pay the costs so they had a beautiful place to worship, and we had financial help paying for the huge building which was more than double in size. I remember that year as people, all types of people donating their willingness to do something. Girls were doing cement patching, as the foreman trained us. There were men who were skilled in woodwork and carpentry who gave of their talents. Many people would come at lunch or at supper and bring us food. They cooked for us and all of it was a freewill offering.

Moses was instructed specially about the freewill offering. It must be voluntary and it must be without blemish. The people of Israel who wanted to give, would give. The gift had to be excellent. It was a special offering unto God.

Leviticus 22: 17 The Lord spoke to Moses, saying: 18 Speak to Aaron, and to his sons, and to all the children of Israel, and say to them: Whoever from the house of Israel or from the foreigners in Israel who offers his burnt offering for any vows or freewill offerings that he offers to the Lord, 19 then if it is to be accepted for you, the offering shall be a male without blemish, a bull, sheep, or goat. 20 But whatever has a blemish you shall not offer, for it shall not be acceptable for you. 21 Whoever offers a sacrifice of peace offerings to the Lord to fulfill his vow or a freewill offering, whether from the herd or flock, to be accepted it shall be perfect, with no blemish on it.

Leviticus 23: 38 besides the Sabbaths of the Lord, besides your gifts, besides all your vows, and besides all your freewill offerings which you give to the Lord,

Freewill offering

I would compare it to buying a special gift for your spouse or your friends. It is not expected; it is completely voluntary and you are giving your best. It doesn't have to only be financial. It can be praise and worship. As part of our regular church meetings we would sometimes have days of prayer and fasting. We would give ourselves to God in a special way as a gift to Him. I've part of several prayer meetings where intercessors would gather and hundreds of prayer requests would come in. We would go pray, praise and then pray over the prayer requests praying for miracles, salvation, healing, deliverance. We gave ourselves as vessels of God to pray and intercede for others. We were 'standing in the gap' (Ezekiel 22: 30). We were praying God's will to be done on earth. We were offering all we had to care for people we may never meet or know.

Praise and worship are also ways of giving freewill offerings to God. I always explain to any new believer he or she should pray and praise God every day. It is a way of drawing closer to God. The truth is though, it is voluntary; you give yourself. There is no formula saying how much you should give or why. You do it because of sincere desire to honour God in a special way.

Psalm 54: 6I will freely sacrifice unto thee: I will praise thy name, O LORD; for it is good.

International House of prayer in Kansas City Missouri is a place that has 24/7 365 prayer and praise and worship. They started in 1999. It has grown to a large congregation of people who come to intercede for others, come to worship and praise God. There are also excellent preaching and teaching sessions. There is a Bible College. They have huge outreaches each year where more than 20 thousand teens and 20's and 30's attend for praise and worship and prayer and learning about God. The worship is excellent because the worshippers live what they sing. They have given themselves to honour God by giving their lives to praise and worship and living wholly unto God. They raise their own finances to be prayer and praise missionaries. Many of them sell CDS and books and get income from it. There are thousands of them. They are training people all over United States and Canada and the world to pray and to worship. They are starting International Houses of Prayer in different places. God TV has donated a channel to livestream the prayer room. Praise and worship and prayer is broadcast 24/7 on it. There are several types of prayer rooms all of them with people committed to prayer and praise.

When I first heard of it, I did not understand the value. I know prayer and praise is important but giving all your life to it – I did not understand because I usually prayed and worshipped and went to church gatherings but I did not do it as lavishly as I had read about the worshippers of IHOP.
Because God is merciful, He has revealed His glory to me as I entered into prayer and praise until I realized the treasure of His presence. His Holy Spirit's indwelling presence comes and He uses me to pray not only for myself but for others. God receives my praise as an offering. I give my best because He has always given me His best. I would compare it to the scripture of the woman who anointed Jesus with precious anointment. She gave the most costly thing she had. It may have been used as a dowry. It could have been sold for a high price. She poured it over Jesus because she wanted to give the best to Him. She recognized His worth.

Matthew 26: 6 When Jesus was in Bethany in the house of Simon the leper, 7 a woman came to Him having an alabaster jar of very expensive ointment and poured it on His head as He sat at supper. 8 When His disciples saw it, they were indignant, saying, "For what purpose is this waste? 9 This ointment might have been sold for a large sum and given to the poor." 10 When Jesus perceived it, He said to them, "Why do you trouble the woman? She has done a good work for Me. 11 For you have the poor always with you, but you do not always have Me. 12 In pouring this ointment on My body, she did it for My burial. 13 Truly I say to you, wherever this gospel shall be preached in the whole world, what this woman has done will be told in memory of her."

She gave her best. Some there noticed she wasn't one of them. Some there, saw her wasting a fortune. Jesus saw her a worshipper and received her gift and blessed her with words that put her in scripture that wherever the gospel is preached, it should be told of how she loved him and gave all in her offering. If we truly give ourselves wholly unto God, He will receive it as an offering.

Apostle Paul

The Apostle Paul, a Hebrew and Greek scholar and Pharisee gave up all to preach Jesus and travel throughout Europe planting churches. He gave his life. He talks about him giving the preaching and teaching as a freewill offering. He also mentions, He is compelled to give for the gospel.

1 Corinthians 9: 16 Though I preach the gospel, I have nothing to boast of, for the requirement is laid upon me. Yes, woe unto me if I do not preach the gospel! 17 So if I do this willingly, I have a reward, but if against my will, I have been entrusted with a commission. 18 What is my reward then? Truly that when I preach the gospel, I may present the gospel of Christ without charge, so that I may not abuse my authority in the gospel.

The apostle Paul took freewill offerings in the churches he planted. They gave willingly. This is not instead of the tithe. It is a freewill offering. It means giving the best; it means giving voluntarily.

1 Corinthians 16: 2 On the first day of the week let every one of you lay in store, as God has prospered him, so that no collections be made when I come.

7 VOW

Chapter 7

A vow is a solemn promise to God. It is stronger than an oath which is a promise to people or a pledge of allegiance. A vow to God means on your life's blood you promise to do something for God. It is like a covenant. It is a promise that cannot be broken.

Marriage is a covenant relationship. In a marriage, the man, the woman and God are in the covenant. The man and woman promise to be devoted to each other for all of their lives. It has been a lifetime commitment. The traditional marriage ceremony involves communion as well as an exchange of vows. Many people write their own vows today. Often marriage is trivialized into a decision that is quickly made and broken. The people have not given themselves wholly to each other or to God.

Not keeping the marriage covenant sacred or precious is not new. The Pharisees tried to trick Jesus into going against scripture. They questioned him about marriage. He made clear the terms of a marriage. There were many people who were committing adultery by polygamy and also divorcing their wives for no reason because they did not want to care for them. Jesus explained that the only reason divorce was permitted was the cause of adultery. He did not want to endorse divorce; he only said it was permitted.

Matthew 19: 4 He answered, "Have you not read that He who made them at the beginning 'made them male and female,'[a] 5 and said, 'For this reason a man shall leave his father and mother and be joined to his wife, and the two shall become one flesh'[b]? 6 So they are no longer two, but one flesh. Therefore what God has joined together, let no man put asunder." 7 They said to Him, "Then why did Moses command to give a certificate of divorce, and to send her away?"[c]
8 He said to them, "Moses, for the hardness of your hearts, permitted you to divorce your wives, but from the beginning it was not so. 9 But I say to you, whoever divorces his wife, except for sexual immorality, and marries another, commits adultery. And whoever marries her who is divorced commits adultery."

Life after divorce

Please, if you have been the victim of a bad marriage situation that has ended in separation or divorce, be encouraged. God is merciful and can renew your life. It is possible that God can lead you to a different type of life. There may be someone in your future that will become your friend, partner for life. Divorce without reason is unacceptable. If you do not truly love the person, do not marry. If you have or are enduring abuse in your marriage, you should get out of it. It is not God's will for you to suffer. The husband should love the wife as God loves the Church. The wife should honour and love her husband as the Church loves Christ. It is a mutual situation where two people are exclusive in their devotion for life. They should respect, honour and care for each other.

The Joining (taken from my book on the Sacraments)

The words used indicate a coming together of lives. They both agree their lives will be lived together. A person should not lightly enter into such an agreement with any person let alone God Himself. In Christian marriage, God is welcomed and present in the ceremony. The two people are not only making their vows to one another but also with God. Such a commitment is sacred. It is the joining of two lives for the glory of God with God as the witness. It literally means they ask God to be in the midst of the marriage. It means both the man and the woman respect God as the leader of the home. They agree to live according to God's Word and to honour each other with their words, actions and lives for all of their lives. God as the head of the home means the Word of God is honored above feelings or disagreements. Both of them, agree to keep God as the centre of their marriage.

Marriage is a most serious commitment. In the Old Testament, a man could not be called into the army if he recently married. He had to stay at home for one year before he could enlist. A man could not make other commitments within that first year of marriage.

Deuteronomy 24: 5 When a man has taken a new wife, he shall not go out to war or be charged with any business; he is to be free at home one year, and must bring joy to his wife which he has taken.

The new testament mentioning of marriage does not change from God's original speaking to Moses. The husbands and wives are to respect and honour each other in their relationship with God and with each other. Jesus is the example given. Just as Christ the head and Saviour of the

Church, suffered and died to redeem His bride, the Church, so should a man love his wife. The husband should be willing to lay down his life to protect and care for his wife. The wife should submit to her husband. I know the word submit releases all kinds of groanings in both women and men. As a single person, you submit to God and your parents. Submit is not a negative word. It means you agree with them

Ephesians 5: 22 Wives, be submissive to your own husbands as unto the Lord. 23 For the husband is the head of the wife, just as Christ is the head and Savior of the church, which is His body. 24 But as the church submits to Christ, so also let the wives be to their own husbands in everything.

A person is never to submit to ungodly treatment by his or her spouse. A person is not to submit to abuse of any kind. A person is not to submit to anything less than Jesus' example of someone who lays down his life to care for his spouse. Jesus ransomed His Bride, the Church, through His love that compelled him to suffer, die and rise from the dead so we could be free from sin and its curse. Jesus is returning to earth one day soon; He is coming as a Bridegroom for His Bride, the Church. God compares the most sacred relationship we have with our Saviour and the hope of His return to a marriage. That means God considers marriage to be sacred. In both living for Jesus Christ and living in a marriage, the two become one. We are to become one with God for all of eternity.

Marriage is spiritual

If you are married to the right person, God will speak to that person concerning you. If you do not know it is the right person, you should never marry that person. God can give words of wisdom, words of knowledge and words of prophecy concerning your life to your spouse. That is not only one way. I know many women who God has spoken to and given spiritual wisdom to speak to their husbands because God sees the marriage as one family unit. The husband is to love his wife as he loves himself. That means he will do everything possible to give the best and the choicest to his wife. He would care about her desires as well as her gifts.

Ephesians 5: 25 Husbands, love your wives, just as Christ also loved the church and gave Himself for it, 26 that He might sanctify and cleanse it with the washing of water by the word, 27 and that He might present to Himself a glorious church, not having spot, or wrinkle, or any such thing, but that it should be holy and without blemish. 28 In this way men ought to love their wives as their own bodies. He who loves his wife loves himself. 29 For no one ever hated his own flesh, but nourishes and cherishes it, just as the Lord cares for the church. 30 For we are members of His body, of His flesh and of His bones. 31 "For this reason a man shall leave his father and mother and shall be joined to his wife, and the two shall be one flesh."[a] 32 This is a great mystery, but I am speaking about Christ and the church. 33 However, let each one of you love his wife as himself, and let the wife see that she respects her husband.

Love for your wife

One of the best descriptions of a husband's love for his wife that I have heard is Mahesh Chavda speak about God dealing very seriously with him about not only letting his wife explore her gifts and talents but encouraging her to use her gifts and talents. He wept as he said God showed him how much God loved her and her spiritual growth was a top priority. He caused him to change in how he saw her. He should pray for her not only with her. She should pray for him and with him. In this way, they will be honouring God and each other.

The man and the woman should encourage and strengthen each other. In this scripture both the husband and wife are commanded to submit to each other. There is equality in their relationship. There is the promise that neither the husband nor the wife would treat the other less than his or herself. A wise woman knows her husband cares for her spiritually and she should listen to what he is speaking to her. A wise husband knows that his wife has special insight and care for him like no other person on earth. They are made to complement each other as a whole.

Ephesians 5: 20 Give thanks always for all things to God the Father in the name of our Lord Jesus Christ, 21 being submissive to one another in the fear of God.

You should marry because you believe God has brought that person into your life and that you would be complimentary to each other, helping each other and strengthening each other. You should marry because you believe that person would be a good parent to your children. You should know without a doubt the person respects and honours and cherishes you. Certainly, there will be physical attraction; there will be spiritual attraction etc. Husbands and wives should build each other up spiritually. They should speak and pray scripture over each other.

Ephesians 5: 26 that He might sanctify and cleanse it with the washing of water by the word, 27 and that He might present to Himself a glorious church, not having spot, or wrinkle, or any such thing, but that it should be holy and without blemish. 28 In this way men ought to love their wives as their own bodies. He who loves his wife loves himself.

Your relationship should be spiritual in that you encourage each other to be the best possible. This would include praying for each other's gifts and talents and success as though you were praying for yourself. Normally the wife gets special intuition about things, and if she is a godly woman, she is praying about them and speaking to her husband about it.

Responsible for the divorce

If you know that you were responsible for the divorce, repent. Turn to God. God promises to forgive any sin we confess if we truly mean it. God can help you live your life. It is possible for God to restore your marriage or for you to enjoy life beyond divorce. Once you receive God's forgiveness, you will truly know freedom from the past situation.

1 John 1: 9 If we confess our sins, He is faithful and just to forgive us our sins and cleanse us from all unrighteousness.

Vow to God in severe circumstances

There is an old movie that is especially precise on making a vow to God. There is a person who survives a shipwreck but is in the middle of the ocean with no help. He makes a vow to God that he will live for God completely if God will just get him out. What happens is that he spots a coastline in the distance and the closer he gets to the shore, the more he tells God that perhaps it will be later in his life that he will be devout and he breaks his vow to give his life to God. It was a humorous situation but many people do something like it. They make vows to God but don't keep them. As soon as the situation turns for the best, they revoke their promises to God.

Making a vow to God

God gave Moses specific instruction on making a vow to God. It involved giving an offering of money or animal etc.

Leviticus 27: And the Lord spoke to Moses, saying: 2 Speak to the children of Israel, and say to them: When a man makes a special vow to the Lord based on the equivalent value[a] of persons, 3 then the equivalent value of a male from twenty to sixty years old shall be fifty shekels[b] of silver, according to the sanctuary shekel.[c] 4 If the person is a female, then the equivalent value shall be thirty shekels.[d] 5 If the person is five to twenty years old, then the equivalent value shall be twenty shekels[e] for a male and ten shekels[f] for a female. 6 If the person is one month to five years old, then the equivalent value shall be five shekels[g] for a male and three shekels[h] of silver for a female. 7 If the person is sixty years old or older, then the equivalent value shall be fifteen shekels[i] for a male and ten shekels for a female. 8 But if he is too poor to afford the equivalent value, then he shall present himself before the priest and the priest shall set his value. According to what the person making the vow can afford, so the priest shall set his value.

If the person wanted, he or she could give his home or property. The person may make a specific vow more than what was required. In the year of Jubilee (every 50th year) it could be redeemed. The person could buy it back. The person would give a gift to God to redeem it. The thing given as a token of the vow was considered Holy. The person was making a special vow for a particular reason that was private between that person and God.

Leviticus 27: 28 Anything that a man shall devote to the Lord from all that he has, whether human, animal, or land, shall not be sold or redeemed. Every devoted thing is most holy to the Lord.

Vow to God as a promise

The prophet Samuel's mother Hanna made a special vow to God. She wanted a child but she was barren. She went to the temple and prayed with all her being. She vowed to give her child for God's service if God would bless her with a child. Eli the priest was mostly deaf and mostly blind. He thought she was drunk because of her quiet prayer. She immediately corrected him and told him that she was praying with all her being. He answered kindly and said May God give her the request. Within one year she had her child Samuel who became a mighty prophet in Israel.

1 Samuel 1: 9 So Hannah arose after they had eaten in Shiloh and after they had drunk. Now Eli the priest was sitting on a seat by the door of the tabernacle of the Lord. 10 And she was bitter, and prayed to the Lord, and wept severely. 11 So she made a vow and said, "O Lord of Hosts, if You will indeed look on the affliction of Your maidservant, and remember me and not forget Your maidservant, but will give to Your maidservant a baby boy, then I will give him to the Lord all the days of his life, and no razor shall touch his head."[a]
12 And as she was praying before the Lord, Eli watched her mouth. 13 Now Hannah was speaking in her heart. Her lips were moving, but her

voice was not heard.

She cared for her child until he a toddler. She brought him plus an offering to give thanks to God. She dedicated him to God and let him live with the priest as a Levite. Samuel was raised to honour and serve God all of his life. God allowed Hanna to have other children.

1 Samuel 1: 24 When she had weaned him, she took him up with her with three bulls, one ephah[b] of flour, and a bottle of wine. And she brought him to the house of the Lord in Shiloh, though the boy was young. 25 Then they slaughtered a bull, and they brought the boy to Eli. 26 And she said, "Oh, my lord! As you live, my lord, I am the woman that stood by you here praying to the Lord. 27 For this boy I prayed, and the Lord has given me my petition which I asked of Him. 28 Therefore also I have let the Lord have him. As long as he lives he will be dedicated to the Lord." And he worshipped the Lord there.

Vow as a Nazarite

There were special people who would dedicate themselves to prayer and serving God wholly for a period of their lives. It was taking the vow of a Nazarite. The person would separate himself from others in prayer and worship to God. The person mostly likely was fasting and praying for a specific situation or to pray for others. The person decided the duration. There were certain rules. the person should be removed from normal life – withdrawn to pray and seek God.

Numbers 6: 1 And the Lord spoke to Moses, saying: 2 Speak to the children of Israel and say to them: When either a man or woman will make a hard vow, the vow of a Nazirite, to separate themselves to the Lord, 3 he will separate himself from wine and strong drink and will drink no vinegar of wine, or vinegar of strong drink. Neither shall he drink any juice of grapes, nor eat fresh or dry grapes. 4 All the days of his separation he will eat nothing that is made of the grapevine, from the seed to the skin.
5 All the days of the vow of his separation no razor will come on his head until the days are fulfilled in which he separates himself to the Lord. He will be holy and will let the locks of the hair of his head grow. 6 All the days that he separates himself to the Lord he will not approach a dead body. 7 He will not defile himself for his father or for his mother, for his brother or for his sister if they die because the separation of his God is on his head. 8 All the days of his separation he is holy to the Lord.

Once the duration of the separation was done, the person was to bring a separate offering to the Temple to complete his or her separation. It involved offering a sacrifice. It involved shaving his or her hair off. It was an outward symbol that the period of special consecration had ended.

Numbers 6: 13 This is the law of the Nazirite. When the days of his separation are fulfilled, he will be brought to the door of the tent of meeting. 14 And he will offer his offering to the Lord, one male lamb a year old without blemish as a burnt offering, one ewe lamb a year old without blemish as a sin offering, one ram without blemish as a peace offering, 15 a basket of unleavened bread, loaves of fine flour mixed with oil, unleavened wafers anointed with oil, and their grain offering with their drink offerings.

16 The priest will bring them before the Lord and will offer his sin offering and his burnt offering. 17 And he will offer the ram as a sacrifice of a peace offering to the Lord with the basket of unleavened bread. The priest will offer also his grain offering and his drink offering.

18 The Nazirite will shave his consecrated head at the door of the tent of meeting, and will take the hair from his consecrated head and put it in the fire which is under the sacrifice of the peace offerings.

19 The priest will take the cooked shoulder of the ram, and one unleavened cake out of the basket, and one unleavened wafer and will put them on the hands of the Nazirite, after he has shaved his consecrated hair. 20 And the priest will wave them as a wave offering before the Lord. This is holy for the priest, with the breast waved and the shoulder offered. And after that the Nazirite may drink wine.

21 This is the law of the Nazirite who has vowed to the Lord, his offering for his separation, besides whatever else his hand is able to provide. According to the vow which he spoke, so he must do, according to the law of his separation.

The Apostle Paul took such a vow during his last trip to Jerusalem. He was going to complete his vow by going to the Temple.

Women making vows – in Leviticus

Women who were living with their dads or husbands were first accountable to them. If they made vows that the dad or the husband did not approve of, she could be set free from the vow. God would forgive her for not keeping it (Numbers 30). A woman who was widowed or divorced or on her own was completely accountable to keep her vow. She could not end it.

Numbers 30: 9 But every vow of a widow and of her that is divorced, with which she has bound herself, will stand against her.

Vow to God to a Church

In some denominations, there are requirements of a member to make certain vows such as abstinence from sex, drugs, and alcohol. The person who makes such a vow is accountable to God if the person breaks the vow. The main theme of the teaching on vows is to never enter into a vow lightly. It is you pledging on your life to do something as unto God.

Jesus warning about making vows

Jesus warns his disciples and those he was teaching not to take vows because many people were sinning against God by making them and breaking them. A vow is sacred.

Matthew 5: 33 "Again, you have heard that it was said by the ancients, 'You shall not swear falsely, but shall fulfill your oaths to the Lord.'[e] 34 But I say to you, do not swear at all: neither by heaven, for it is God's throne; 35 nor by the earth, for it is His footstool; nor by Jerusalem, for it is the city of the great King. 36 Nor shall you swear by your head, because you cannot make one hair white or black. 37 But let your 'Yes' mean 'Yes,' and 'No' mean 'No.' For whatever is more than these comes from the evil one.
Benny Hinn

I heard an excellent teaching by Benny Hinn on making a vow and keeping it. I have not heard much teaching on the subject; most of what I received is my own Bible study and experience. Benny Hinn was born in Israel; their family was praying for a miracle of approval to move to Canada. The situation was not easy. Benny Hinn, promised God to bring a huge can of oil to the church (as was used in the church) if God would grant them special favour. What occurred is that they did receive their approval to go to Canada and Benny Hinn was reminded by God of his vow and he kept it. He gave the offering to the church as he promised.

My mother

I was a teenager and quite close to my mother. She had arthritis and pseudolithiasis. What it meant is she was often in pain. Humidity affected her. Weather affected her. She could feel in her body if it was going to storm. She knew because it affected her. One summer, she was bedridden in pain. She was praying and praying. She did not play with us or do much with us. It went on for several weeks of pain. She had made a special vow to God that she would quit smoking if God raised her up. Within a short period, she was up and walking around and cleaning and cooking and being her normal self. She was a Jehovah witness. She did not have Bible studies for several weeks because of her pain.

One day, the Jehovah witnesses came and my mother welcomed them. They talked and prayed. The one Jehovah witness asked how her health improved. My mother confessed it was God who healed her because she had made a special vow to quit smoking. The lady asked if she had kept the vow. My mother admitted no she had not. My mother would quit smoking one day or 1 week and always go back to it. The Jehovah witness told her that she must keep her vow because God answered her prayer and she would be directly sinning against God by not keeping it.

I am not a Jehovah witness; I am a Christian, but the woman spoke the truth to her about her vow. My mother realized she made a vow that could not be broken. She prayed asking God to help her because she knew she could not do it. She quit smoking immediately and never went back to it. Later she became a Spirit filled Christian.

Vow

I do not recommend making vows unless you would die for it. Making a vow means you lay your life on the line. Breaking a Vow means direct sin against God. If you have promised something, you must give it to God.

8 FIRST FRUIT OFFERING

Chapter 8

The first fruits offering was first established by God choosing Aaron and all his family to be Levitical priests to God. God chose them and their descendants to be set apart from all of the other tribes. They had to devote their lives to service the Tabernacle and the offerings and tithes of the people. They were to teach the people all the commandments. They were holy, chosen, and different. They did not own property or have an inheritance as other tribes. God gave them a portion of the tithes and offerings instead.

Exodus 28: 1 And bring near to yourself Aaron, your brother, and his sons with him from among the children of Israel, so that they may minister to Me as priests—Aaron, Nadab and Abihu, Eleazar and Ithamar, Aaron's sons. 2

An offering of all things including consecrating the first-born children, were to be given to God. People and animals could be redeemed by making a payment or giving an offering in its place.

Exodus 22: 29 You must give to Me the firstborn of your sons. 30 Likewise you must do the same with your oxen and with your sheep. Seven days it shall remain with its mother, but on the eighth day you must give it to Me.

Israel's first giving

Israel had been delivered out of Egyptian slavery after 400 years. God gave special instructions to them as they inherited their land. It was the first that they could grow their own crops in their own land. It was the first that their herds would multiply in their new land. God gave special instructions to them so they would honour God and remember their inheritance. They would remember the commandments and the miracles that God had done for them.

First, they were to gather the first fruits meaning the first of their crops or animals or livelihood.

Deuteronomy 26: 1 And it must be, when you come into the land which the

Lord your God is giving you for an inheritance, and you possess it, and dwell in it, 2 that you shall take from the first of all the produce of the ground which you shall bring from your land that the Lord your God is giving you, and put it in a basket and go to the place where the Lord your God chooses to make His name abide.

Next, they were to bring the firstfruits to the priest as honour to God. It showed they knew God had given them the promised land. They knew it was God who kept His covenant with Abraham, with Moses and with Joshua. They knew they came from slaves who served Egypt. They knew that God delivered them and gave them the land he had promised them. Each first fruit offering was a reminder to them of the miracles God had done for them. It was an oral tradition of passing on the faith.

Deuteronomy 26: 3 You shall go to the priest in office at that time and say to him, "I profess this day to the Lord your God that I have come into the land which the Lord promised to our fathers to give us." 4 The priest will take the basket out of your hand and set it down before the altar of the Lord your God. 5 Then you must answer and say before the Lord your God, "A wandering Aramean[a] was my father, and he went down into Egypt, and sojourned there with only a few in number, but there he became a great, mighty, and populous nation. 6 However, the Egyptians mistreated and afflicted us, and laid upon us harsh labor. 7 And when we cried to the Lord God of our fathers, the Lord heard our voice, and looked on our affliction, our labor, and our oppression. 8 And the Lord brought us forth out of Egypt with a mighty hand and with an outstretched arm and with great terror, and with signs and wonders.

They acknowledged God's provision. They confessed their faith in God's giving them the promised land and the fertility of the land as well as their herds. It was an expression of devotion and thanksgiving giving the first, giving the best.

Deuteronomy 26: 9 Then He brought us into this place, and has given us this land, a land that flows with milk and honey. 10 Now, indeed, I have brought the first fruits of the land, which you, O Lord, have given me." Then you must set it before the Lord your God and worship before the Lord your God. 11 You must rejoice in every good thing which the Lord your God has given to you and your house, you, and the Levite, as well as the foreigner who is among you.

They confessed that they had given the tithes and cared for the poor as they were commanded.

Deuteronomy 26: 12 When you have finished tithing all the tithes of your income the third year, which is the year of tithing, and have given it to the Levite, the foreigner, the orphan, and the widow, that they may eat within your towns and be satisfied, 13 then you shall say before the Lord your God, "I have removed the sacred things out of my house and also have given them to the Levite, and to the foreigner, to the orphan, and to the widow, according to all Your commandments which You have commanded me. I have not transgressed Your commandments or forgotten them.

Offering the First Fruits

God gave specific commandment to Moses on how to give the offering.

Leviticus 23: 9 The Lord spoke to Moses, saying: 10 Speak to the children of Israel, and say to them: When you have come into the land that I am giving to you and reap its harvest, then you shall bring a sheaf bundle of the first fruits of your harvest to the priest. 11 And he shall wave the sheaf before the Lord so that you may be accepted. On the day after the Sabbath the priest shall wave it. 12 You shall offer that day when you wave the sheaf a year-old male lamb without blemish for a burnt offering to the Lord. 13 The grain offering shall be two-tenths of an ephah[a] of wheat flour mixed with oil, a food offering made by fire to the Lord for a pleasing aroma; its drink offering shall be of wine, a fourth of a hin.[b] 14 You shall eat neither bread nor grain, parched or fresh, until the same day that you have brought an offering to your God. It shall be a perpetual statute throughout your generations in all your dwellings.

They confessed that they rejoiced at God's provision and made petition for God to receive their first fruits offering. Part of the celebration of giving was to feast during the giving. It was an act of worship. It was a season of rejoicing at God's provision. Although there is no mention of first fruits giving in the New covenant, it is still practiced by many Christians. There are many popular teachers and preachers who teach on the giving of first fruits, primarily because God never revoked it. God di not say it was not necessary any more. What it is honouring God with your substance or finances to thank Him for increase or promotion or special inheritance.

Deuteronomy 26: 14 I have not eaten anything when in mourning, nor have I removed anything while unclean, nor offered anything to the dead. I have listened to the voice of the Lord my God and have done according to all that You have commanded me. 15 Look down from Your holy habitation, from heaven, and bless Your people Israel and the land which You have given us, as You swore to our fathers, a land flowing with milk and honey."

Each year as the crops were increased or more than the previous year, an offering of the increase was given as the first fruits. It was an annual celebration. To apply it to today, you would give a portion of your raise or promotion. You would give a special offering of your increase.

Nehemiah 10: 35 and, likewise, for the annual bringing of the first fruits of our ground and the first fruits of all fruit of all trees to the house of the Lord; 36 and for bringing to the priests who are ministering at the house of God, the firstborn of our sons and livestock, as it is written in the Law, plus the firstborn of our herds and flocks.

The firstfruits were to be given to the Levites because they were the tribes of priests that God had chosen to inherit them. They offered up the sacrifices and offerings according to the Levitical laws that God spoke to Moses.

Nehemiah 10: 37 Moreover, the first of our fresh dough, our contributions, the fruit of every tree, and the new wine and oil we will bring to the priests at the chambers of the house of our God, but the tithe of our crops we will bring to the Levites, since they themselves receive the tithes in all our agricultural cities.

There is a special blessing on all giving to God. God promises to fill your barns and presses. There is an overflow of abundance. God is a God who continuously blesses you. The blessings increase year by year. First fruits is a way of keeping your heart right with God. Rather than let covetousness or pride enter into a person's heart, giving God the increase shows that you truly know him as your source and you honour him by giving of the increase. It is a sure way to keep your heart fixed on God rather than on money, crops, things or blessings.

Proverbs 3: 9 Honor the Lord with your substance,
    and with the first fruits of all your increase;
10 so your barns will be filled with plenty,
    and your presses will burst out with new wine.

Money is not the root of all evil. God prospers His people. God's delight is to bless and increase his people beyond what they have known because He is a generous giver and a good God. The love of money is the root of all evil (1 Timothy 6: 10). If a person focuses on what blessings God has given to him or believes that he himself is the source of the blessing, most certainly he is filled with the sin of pride and will come to ruin.

Any believer who does not honour God as the origin of all of creation or the source of all blessings, is directly sinning against God. Jesus warned of covetousness and self – importance. Focusing on your blessing and not God who gave you the blessing is sin. It is making an idol of money or wealth. Jesus told the parable about the rich man who was content within himself and gave no thought to God or other people. He simply planned to get more. Covetousness can be described as a lust for more. Wanting more is not wrong – but respecting God first in giving and others who are poor or needy is central to the Christian (Judaic) Faith.

Luke 12: 16 And He told a parable to them, saying, "The land of a rich man produced plentifully. 17 He thought to himself, 'What shall I do, for I have no room to store my crops?'

18 "Then he said, 'This I will do: I will pull down my barns and build greater ones, and there I will store all my grain and my goods. 19 And I will say to my soul, Soul, you have many goods laid up for many years. Take rest. Eat, drink, and be merry.'

20 "But God said to him, 'You fool! This night your soul will be required of you. Then whose will those things be which you have provided?'

21 "So is he who stores up treasure for himself, and is not rich toward God."

Even non-believers who do not honour God and are filled with pride in self and think themselves as god will come to ruin. King Nebuchadnezzar became full of pride as he saw his kingdom and all the glory of it. He foolishly believed he was responsible for all of it. He thought pride within himself and believed he was like a god. Judgement came upon him because of it. God spoke to him in correction and said that as soon as he respected God has his creator he would be restored. He was transformed so that he resembled an animal and he wandered like an animal for 7 years.

Daniel 4: 28 All this came upon King Nebuchadnezzar. 29 At the end of twelve months he walked on the roof of the palace of the kingdom of Babylon. 30 The king spoke, saying, "Is this not Babylon the Great that I myself have built as a royal residence by my mighty power and for the honor of my majesty?"

Daniel 4:31 While the word was in the king's mouth, there fell a voice from heaven: "O King Nebuchadnezzar, to you it is spoken: The kingdom has departed from you! 32 And you shall be driven away from men, and your dwelling shall be with the animals of the field. You shall be given grass to eat as oxen, and seven periods of time shall pass over you until you know that the Most High rules over the kingdom of men and gives it to whomever He wills."

Daniel 4:33 Immediately the thing was fulfilled concerning Nebuchadnezzar. And he was driven from men and ate grass as oxen, and his body was wet with the dew of heaven until his hairs were grown like eagles' feathers and his nails like birds' claws.

After 7 years, he suddenly recognized God as being the creator and gave him glory. As he worshipped God, he came to his senses and miraculously his kingdom was restored to him.

Daniel 4: 34 But at the end of the days, I, Nebuchadnezzar, lifted up my eyes to heaven, and my understanding returned to me, and I blessed the Most High, and I praised and honored Him who lives forever:

For His dominion is an everlasting dominion,
    and whose kingdom endures from generation to generation.
35 And all the inhabitants of the earth
    are reputed as nothing;
and He does according to His will
    in the army of heaven
    and among the inhabitants of the earth.
And no one can stay His hand or say to Him,
    "What have You done?"

36 At the same time my reason returned to me. And for the glory of my kingdom, my honor and splendor returned to me.

Truly heart attitude matters to God with all giving. We should give our best. We should give because we know God has provided for us. We should give as an expression of worship to God.

The first fruits is giving the first, the best and that declared holy by God.

In 1 Corinthians 15, the apostle Paul refers to Jesus as the first fruits back from the dead. What he is doing is comparing the resurrection of Christ to the first fruits offering that the people knew about. Jesus Christ was the first; our faith in Christ is what assures us of resurrection life. We believe that as Jesus died and rose from the dead, so shall we who believe in Christ. It is the core doctrine of the Christian faith.

Romans 11: 16 For if the first fruit be holy, the lump is also holy: and if the root be holy, so are the branches.

Jesus, is the first, the best, the most Holy. It is an excellent analogy because Jesus truly was God giving His best to us. He gave Jesus so that we who believe might be saved. Jesus was completely holy; he never sinned; that is why he could die on the cross for us. He could take our place because he never sinned. He lived Holy. He had no inherited sin. Jesus is the resurrection and the life. He said it and he proved it by his resurrection from the dead.

John 11: 25 Jesus said to her, "I am the resurrection and the life. He who believes in Me, though he may die, yet shall he live. 26 And whoever lives and believes in Me shall never die. Do you believe this?"

First fruits is not only an offering but is a principle of life. The first, the best, the most wonderful, God gives to us. We give Him our first, our best, our choicest. If we truly keep this principle in our lives, we will never be prideful or arrogant. We honour God, our heart is free from covetousness. God can prosper us and bless us more and more because our character remains humble and our faith in God as the source is the foundation of our lives.

9 CONCLUSION ON GIVING

Chapter 9

It was my desire to write the teaching on giving because I believe many people who go to church regularly, do not get teaching on the different types of giving. The teaching is not to entangle you in any way. If you don't feel the release in your spirit in any area of the teaching, may God bless you; do what you know to do.

The teaching is not to try to legislate giving. The book is written to give you understanding on different types of Biblical giving based on the scriptures so that you may prosper.

A scriptural explanation on the types of giving, is meant to inform you so that as you prosper, you will begin to give to the kingdom of God. As God increases you, you will think of others and desire to help people.

Tithes
Alms
Sowing a seed
Thanksgiving offering
Free will offering
First fruits offering

You can give all of the above types of giving, but if you do not respect God as the source of all blessing and honour Him as Creator and Saviour, you will not honour God with your giving. Giving to God is important but the attitude of the heart is most important. Giving to God because He is God – the origin of all of creation. Giving to God because He has prospered you, Giving to God because He has given you the best is not a bondage; it is the opposite. Giving means you are free. Being a generous giver means you are not ensnared with money or wealth. It means God can trust you with more finances or more wealth.

Enough

I have heard people that say, I don't want to be a millionaire; I only want enough for me and my family. Although that may sound religiously correct, it is really selfish. If God prospers you, it is so you can give more. Please see your life although very important is not the only consideration. There are millions of people who do not yet know Christ. The non-Christians are not going to finance the preaching of the gospel. Those who give to the gospel are those who know its value. If God should prosper you beyond your needs, it is so you can give more. You can help care for poor or widows or orphans. You can give special gifts to missions or support a ministry you receive teaching from. God blesses us, so we can be a blessing.

Should you be a tithing Christian, God is going to prosper you. You are going to increase: to many it may be financial; to some may be in people giving to you; to some may be in special favour over your life. You are not the end of the blessing; you are blessed so that you may pass on the blessing. Giving is a way of life. Your loose grip on the wealth God gives you, the more God can entrust to flow through your hands to bless others. Yes, God wants to supply all your needs. Yes, God will even give you the desires of your heart.

God also desires people he can entrust to finances the preaching of the gospel. There is a call for those who would give unto God as a partner with Holy spirit. God wants people he can entrust to care for the poor and needy who could never repay you. As you give in faith and in prayer, God may allow finances beyond your imagination to flow through your hands. Should you keep your heart right, honouring God, He can use you to be a vessel He can use in giving. God may speak to your spirit about giving to certain people. God may speak to you about giving to certain ministries or certain organizations. The Holy Spirit will direct you so that your giving will become the answer to someone's prayers. It would be a partnership with God - the Holy Spirit directing you in direct partnership with God in the gift of giving.

Please consider the teaching for your own self and how it can apply to your life. Also, please consider offering yourself as a giver. Commit yourself to God and let Him direct your giving. Offer your finances, your possessions, your talents, all He has given you. Say God, if you want to use me to give, give me the request, provide the finances and I'll give. Offer yourself as a willing vessel. If you do it, your life will never be the same. God will begin to give to you and use you as a vessel He can flow through with giving.

Romans 12: 1 I urge you therefore, brothers, by the mercies of God, that you present your bodies as a living sacrifice, holy, and acceptable to God, which is your reasonable service of worship. 2 Do not be conformed to this world, but be transformed by the renewing of your mind, that you may prove what is the good and acceptable and perfect will of God.

PRAYERS

PRAYERS

The following prayers are samples of prayers you could pray for important reasons. You could pray the same meaning in your own words. The prayers are meant as examples only.

PRAYER FOR SALVATION

Thank you- Jesus that you died for me on the cross. Thank you that you rose from the dead and ascended into heaven. Thank you that you are coming back again. I thank you Jesus for forgiving my sins. Thank you for your blood that cleanses me from all sin and unrighteousness. Thank you that your blood makes me holy. Thank you for saving me. Fill me with the Holy Spirit to overflowing. I pray for the baptism of the Holy Spirit. Lead me to other people who love you and serve you and that can help me know more about you. Give me the discerning of spirits strong. I thank you and praise you. With my mouth, I confess Jesus Christ is my LORD. Amen.

PRAYER FOR BAPTISM OF THE HOLY SPIRIT

Thank you- Jesus that you promised to send the gift of the Holy Spirit to us. Thank you that this promise is to all believers. I am a believer. I want all of you that you will give me. I want to know you God. Baptize me in the Holy Spirit with the evidence of speaking in other tongues. I believe you want to fill me to overflowing with your Spirit so that I might be an effective witness for Christ on the earth. Thank you for saving me. Thank you for your Holy presence. [begin praising God for what He has done for you – sing worship choruses and praise God in your natural language. Believe that He is present with you – start praising and worshipping Him. As phrases come to you in other tongues, say them – praise God with new tongues.] I praise you. I thank you. I receive the baptism of the Holy Spirit.

PRAYER FOR RELEASING ANGELS

God, I thank you that angels are ministering spirits sent as ministers to us. I pray over my prayer request NAME IT HERE. God I pray release angels to perform it. I thank you for releasing the answer to me. I praise you for it. Amen.

PRAYER FOR RESISTING EVIL

I am the redeemed of the LORD. Jesus Christ has saved me. I am a new creation in Christ Jesus. Jesus blood covers me. I live in the spirit. The Holy Spirit of God fills my spirit. O Holy Spirit quicken me; give me wisdom. Pray [expecting God will give you discerning of spirits so you will have the right words to speak.]

In the name of Jesus Christ, I bind you. I rebuke you evil spirit. In the name of Jesus, I command you to go out. You have no place in my life. I cast you out. You have no place with me. I am covered by the blood of Jesus and His righteousness is my righteousness. Go out evil spirit in the name of Jesus Christ!
Thank you, Holy spirit for your holy presence. Release angels to drive out the enemy. Thank you. Amen.

PRAYER FOR PROTECTION

Holy Spirit release angels to protect me. I plead the blood of Jesus over me. I pray the protection you promise to your people. Cover me Jesus. Holy Spirit give me wisdom, discernment and understanding. Thank you for angels that guard over me. Thank you for your blood that protects me and a hedge of protection around me. I praise you O God. [praise God with some worship choruses and expect God's holy presence to be manifest in you]. Thank you. O God for protection.

PRAYER FOR HEALING

Lord Jesus, Thank you that you gave your life for me so that I can be saved, healed and delivered. I thank you for the scripture that by your stripes I am healed. I thank you for my healing.

NAME THE DISEASE I bind you in the name of Jesus. I cast you out. I pray over myself that I would be whole spirit, soul and body.

Thank you, God. for your healing manifestation in my life. I give you all the glory. Amen.

PRAYER OF REPENTENCE

Jesus, thank you for your blood shed for me. I repent of the sin of NAME IT. I thank you for liberty from sin. I cut off the root of iniquity in my family. I thank you for your empowering presence to live a Holy life. Holy Spirit lead and guide me in the paths of righteousness. Thank you for giving me godly desires. Let my life align with your word. In Jesus name. Amen.

Prayer of dedication as a giver

God, thank you for prospering me. Let me be a giver you can use to give to others. God let my character be humble and giving so that you place things and wealth in my hands and I will give as you lead me. If you prosper me with more than enough, I will obey your promptings to give to the gospel, to people and for the glory of God. Use me as a giver. I give myself wholly to you. In Jesus name. Amen.

OTHER BOOKS BY CHRIS LEGEBOW

Available on Amazon.ca Amazon.com or Kindle
Or the Create Space webstore.

Living Word Publishers

Angels: Ministering Spirits

An Excellent Spirit: Living Life Wholly Unto God

Covenant With God: God's Relationship With Man

Discovering and Using your Spiritual Gifts

Divine Healing in the Scriptures: God's Mercy Towards Man

Kinds of Giving: from the Holy Scriptures

The Commandments

The Doctrine of Christ: Essential Truths of Scripture

The Five-Fold Ministry: Gifts to the Church

Kinds of Prayer. Knowing Them and Using Them Effectively

Living Life Fully: Knowing your Purpose

Spiritual Fruit: The Importance of Godly Character

The Anointing: the Glory of God

The High Calling: Life Worth Living

The Sacraments: A Charismatic Guide

ABOUT THE AUTHOR

Chris Legebow is a Christian Professor of English and Communications. She has taught at the elementary, high school and College and University levels. She has ministered in her local churches in intercessory prayer, teaching Sunday school and other Christian Doctrine classes to children and youths. She has preached to congregations and given her testimony. Although she was not raised in a Christian home, she came to know Jesus Christ as her Saviour and LORD while she was studying in University. This radically transformed her life in terms of priorities and commitment.

She has a strong passion for the great commission – that Jesus Christ would be preached throughout all the earth believing that it a major sign of the LORD's return. She has been a part of several different types of full gospel charismatic churches but has also gained much of her insight and enlightenment from Christian Media and broadcasting. She hopes to continue ministering, serving, interceding and giving and teaching until the LORD returns.

www.ingramcontent.com/pod-product-compliance
Lightning Source LLC
Chambersburg PA
CBHW021210020426
42331CB00003B/291